SPACES OF CREATION

After the Empire: The Francophone World and Postcolonial France

Series Editor:
Valérie K. Orlando, University of Maryland

Advisory Board

Robert Bernasconi, Memphis University; Claire H. Griffiths, University of Chester, UK; Alec Hargreaves, Florida State University; Chima Korieh, Rowan University; Mildred Mortimer, University of Colorado, Boulder; Obioma Nnaemeka, Indiana University; Alison Rice, University of Notre Dame; Kamal Salhi, University of Leeds; Tracy D. Sharpley-Whiting, Vanderbilt University; Nwachukwu Frank Ukadike, Tulane University

Recent Titles

Spaces of Creation: Transculturality and Feminine Expression in Francophone Literature, by Allison Connolly

Women Writers of Gabon: Literature and Herstory, by Cheryl Toman

Backwoodsmen as Ecocritical Motif in French Canadian Literature: Connecting Worlds in the Wilds, by Anne Rehill

Intertextual Weaving in the Work of Linda Lê: Imagining the Ideal Reader, by Alexandra Kurmann

Front Cover Iconography and Algerian Women's Writing: Heuristic Implications of the Recto-Verso Effect, by Pamela A. Pears

The Algerian War in French-Language Comics: Postcolonial Memory, History, and Subjectivity, by Jennifer Howell

Writing through the Visual and Virtual: Inscribing Language, Literature, and Culture in Francophone Africa and the Caribbean, edited by Ousseina D. Alidou and Renée Larrier

State Power, Stigmatization, and Youth Resistance Culture in the French Banlieues: Uncanny Citizenship, by Hervé Tchumkam

Violence in Caribbean Literature: Stories of Stones and Blood, by Véronique Maisier

Ousmane Sembene and the Politics of Culture, edited by Lifongo J. Vetinde and Amadou T. Fofana

Reimagining the Caribbean: Conversations among the Creole, English, French, and Spanish Caribbean, edited by Valérie K. Orlando and Sandra Messinger Cypress

Rethinking Reading, Writing, and a Moral Code in Contemporary France: Postcolonializing High Culture in the Schools of the Republic, by Michel Laronde

The French Colonial Imagination: Writing the Indian Uprisings, 1857–1858, from Second Empire to Third Republic, by Nicola Frith

Shifting Perceptions of Migration in Senegalese Literature, Film, and Social Media, by Mahriana Rofheart

The Narrative Mediterranean: Beyond France and the Maghreb, by Claudia Esposito

SPACES OF CREATION

Transculturality and Feminine Expression in Francophone Literature

Allison Connolly

LEXINGTON BOOKS
Lanham • Boulder • New York • London

Published by Lexington Books
An imprint of The Rowman & Littlefield Publishing Group, Inc.
4501 Forbes Boulevard, Suite 200, Lanham, Maryland 20706
www.rowman.com

Unit A, Whitacre Mews, 26-34 Stannary Street, London SE11 4AB

British Library Cataloguing in Publication Information Available

Library of Congress Cataloging-in-Publication Data Available

ISBN 978-1-4985-3936-4 (cloth : alk. paper)
ISBN 978-1-4985-3937-1 (electronic)

∞™ The paper used in this publication meets the minimum requirements of
American National Standard for Information Sciences Permanence of Paper for
Printed Library Materials, ANSI/NISO Z39.48-1992.

Printed in the United States of America

This book is dedicated to my family.

CONTENTS

ABBREVIATIONS

Page references for the texts most often cited in this book include the following abbreviations:

BQ   *Le Bonheur a la queue glissante*, Abla Farhoud

EM   *L'espérance-macadam*, Gisèle Pineau

FS   *La Femme sans sépulture*, Assia Djebar

IG   *L'Ingratitude*, Ying Chen

PP   *Un plat de porc aux bananes vertes*, André and Simone Schwarz-Bart

PV   *Pluie et vent sur Télumée Miracle*, Simone Schwarz-Bart

RA   *Des rêves et des assassins*, Malika Mokeddem

PREFACE

I have always been drawn to narratives of personal transformation. My study of postcolonial literature and French has led me to novels in which marginalized mothers and daughters are unable to easily participate in enriching and dynamic exchanges that occur in the public sphere. In these stories, I discovered women "caught" in undesirable situations—forced to migrate, limited by their romantic entwinements, or ensnared in wars of liberation. Through the years, their stories have incited my compassion and curiosity. I wondered how women in restrictive environments connected to others and nurtured their own transformation. Tangentially, I was also interested in how writing and storytelling might impact their respective paths.

Spaces of Creation: Transculturality and Feminine Expression in Francophone Literature grows from these concerns. My study aims to carve a space for consideration of self-expression by literary mothers and daughters in postcolonial societies. Drawing links between the Francophone literature of Canada, the French Caribbean, and North Africa, I will explore the hypothesis that problematic issues of dynamic, contemporary societies *can* and *do* fuel creative acts on the part of women. I intend to demonstrate that their painful existence provides the opportunity—*the space of creation*—necessary to weave and transmit stories.

ACKNOWLEDGMENTS

Spaces of Creation has grown and lived in me for half my life. Numerous people have nurtured me in this project. I thank my family for always giving me time and space to think, explore, and find my voice. I am grateful to Annette Sampon-Nicolas, who has been a guiding light since the genesis of this project when I was an undergraduate student at Hollins University. At the University of North Carolina at Chapel Hill, Dominique Fisher and Martine Antle provided consistent, rigorous training as I dove into scholarly life. At Centre College, my colleague Ken Keffer inspires me through his creative teaching and scholarship. I am also grateful to my kind and attentive students whose genuine interest in my scholarship has served as a motivating force.

As the years passed and *Spaces of Creation* grew, very good friends provided me with beautiful spaces in which to write: the late Nancy Bryan Faircloth, Wyndham Robertson, and Frédérick Beaujeu-Dufour and Anne Faircloth. Shelley Richardson read an early version of my manuscript and helped me to more clearly articulate the conceptual underpinnings of my work. Leslie Kealhofer-Kemp provided thoughtful commentary for which I am truly grateful. Sara Loy proofread the manuscript, and Bruce Richardson talked me through the intricacies of publishing. I owe a special thanks to Arica Lee James Smith for contributing her artwork to the book cover, as well as to Ben Richardson for photographing the painting.

I am in gratitude to Centre College for sustained support of this project through sabbatical leaves, summer research funding, and the NEH associate professorship in French. At Lexington Books, I thank Lindsey Po-

xiv ACKNOWLEDGMENTS

rambo and Anthony "Nick" Johns for their encouragement and efficiency throughout the review and production process.

The author and publisher are grateful for permission to reproduce the following copyrighted material:

Excerpts from *Le Bonheur a la queue glissante* by Abla Farhoud, copyright © 2004. Reprinted with permission of Groupe Ville-Marie Littérature inc.

Excerpts from *L'espérance macadam* by Gisèle Pineau, copyright © 1995. Reprinted with permission of the author.

Excerpts from *L'Ingratitude* by Ying Chen, copyright © 1995. Lémac Editeur. Reprinted with permission of the author.

Excerpts from *Pluie et vent sur Télumée Miracle* by Simone Schwarz-Bart, copyright © Editions du Seuil 1972, *Points*, 1995. Reprinted with permission of Editions du Seuil.

Excerpts from *Des rêves et des assassins* by Malika Mokeddem, copyright © 1995. Reprinted with permission of Grasset & Fasquelle.

This book is derived in part from my article "Now and Then: Spaces of Oppression in *Un Plat de porc aux bananes vertes*," published in *Contemporary French & Francophone Studies*. September 2011. Copyright © Taylor & Francis.

I

INTRODUCTION

Carving Literary Spaces: Feminine Voices in a Transcultural World

An old and lonely woman withers away in a Paris retirement home. She has lost contact with friends and family in her native Martinique, experiences abject poverty that forces her to beg for money in the street, and endures cruel treatment from her fellow residents. Mariotte, the protagonist in André and Simone Schwarz-Bart's novel *Un plat de porc aux bananes vertes* (1967), embodies the harsh consequences of nomadism and exile, and her troubling story brings to mind the potential loneliness of contemporary urban societies. In her unhappy and unenviable situation, Mariotte attempts to escape from her present by taking refuge in memories from her past and her island. In her intense daydreams, she seeks her beloved mother, yet the family member with whom she most quickly and intensely connects is her vindictive grandmother Man Louise.[1]

Making our way through the novel, we quickly discover that two mother figures reside in Mariotte's imagination: the desired mother who is just out of her imagination's reach and the feared grandmother who returns to chide her now-elderly granddaughter. Throughout *Un plat de porc*, the Schwarz-Barts explore a theme that will weave itself into Francophone literature[2] throughout the rest of the twentieth century and which is of utmost importance in this study: the complex interactions that exist between mothers and daughters in a culturally diverse society.[3]

The topic of mothers in literature, and in particular the relationships between mothers and daughters, has proven to be of scholarly interest in the last decades due to the continued interest in feminist movements and their effects in respective societies. My study has been informed by a number of previous works in literary, cultural, and sociological domains, both in Western and non-Western contexts. Scholarship in Western contexts can be very useful in examination of mothers and motherhood in Francophone postcolonial contexts both in the West and elsewhere, as they often set a precedent of questioning a woman's place in society.[4] Marianne Hirsch's book *The Mother/Daughter Plot: Narrative, Psychoanalysis, Feminism* poses challenging questions pertaining to society's definitions and perceptions of mothers.[5] Likewise, Elisabeth Badinter's books *L'Amour en plus* and *Le conflit: la femme et la mère* challenge maternal status in French society. Previous studies on mother figures in Francophone postcolonial contexts tend to portray mothers as powerful figures in their societies, underlining the positive aspects of relationships between mothers and their children as well as the respected place some mother figures hold. For example, in her interview with Simone Schwarz-Bart, Mary Jean Green emphasizes the mother's central role in the family unit, downplaying many of the challenges faced by mothers in a postcolonial setting. Although she acknowledges the difficult familial situations of many immigrant families in Quebec, Lucie Lequin nonetheless focuses on the mother's role as protector of cultural heritage. The maternal legacy as guardian of tradition overshadows familial and societal conflicts that impact the characters she examines.[6]

Stories about mothers and daughters do not cease to be tantalizing, both in Western and non-Western contexts, perhaps due to the ease with which readers relate to familial ups and downs. As we will see in subsequent chapters, the elderly Mariotte embodies the difficulties experienced by mothers and daughters who find themselves in the economic and linguistic margins of society: discrimination, familial conflict, patriarchal domination, and displacement.[7] The Schwarz-Barts and later authors of the Francophone world create multifaceted mother figures whose strengths and weaknesses are evident in their interaction with their families. They represent various ethnicities, languages, temperaments, and religious backgrounds. Many of these mothers are caring, warm characters. Others are emotionally distant or completely absent from their children's lives. Ying Chen's *L'Ingratitude* (1995) and Abla Farhoud's *Le*

Bonheur a la queue glissante (2004) reveal the pressures of migrant culture in Canada. The French Caribbean's history of forced migration and slavery impact families in the Schwarz-Barts' *Un plat de porc*, Simone Schwarz-Bart's *Pluie et vent sur Télumée Miracle* (1972), and Gisèle Pineau's *L'espérance-macadam* (1995). Contemporary Algerian authors Assia Djebar and Malika Mokkedem depict motherless young women who feel the need to comprehend the traumatisms their mothers suffered before their untimely deaths in *La Femme sans sépulture* (2004) and *Des rêves et des assassins* (1995).

Each of these novels points to both the richness and hardships of family life for those who live with a legacy of colonialism, displacement, or both. My examination of the works as an ensemble serves several purposes. First, I expose commonalities shared by women across the French-speaking world, including isolation and the loss of family members in violent circumstances. Second, I demonstrate that these and other similarities give way to shared concerns spanning generations and borders, such as the agency of women and the preservation of cultural traditions. Third, this study analyzes the culturally dynamic conditions in which contemporary mother and daughter figures evolve, revealing patterns that link characters from different religious and ethnic backgrounds. Given the often lonely circumstances in which immigrant mothers find themselves, how do they carry out their roles of protector, nurturer, and breadwinner? If at all, how do they seek to create and maintain peace within their family? To what extent does symbolic violence influence the relationships of mothers and their daughters? What role, if any, can literature play in voicing the experiences of marginalized women? Why is it relevant and crucial to listen to voices of resistance by women of transcultural communities?

While in no way undermining the positive aspects of mothers and motherhood as they are presented in postcolonial literature in French, I examine the nuances of motherhood in postcolonial contexts so as to demonstrate the complexities of mother figures raising their children in diverse societies. Comparing mother figures within and across different Francophone areas, I take into account the similarities and differences between regions, each of which is influenced by traditions passed from one generation to the next as well as by pressures exerted by a particular postcolonial society.

DIVERSITY AND RESISTANCE

Before undertaking close readings of novels from across the French-speaking world, let us first examine theoretical concepts pertinent to the representation of women, and more specifically, of mother figures. The present study links Creole theories of cultural diversity to current discussions on transculturality, insomuch as they affect mothers and daughters. Wolfgang Welsch's theory of transculturality asserts that contemporary cultures rely on entwinement and influence on a person-to-person level, surpassing identities tied to nation. Where do displaced women fit in his vision of vivid exchange between people? In diverse societies described by Welsch, how do "feminine" identities form and evolve? Do "feminine" literary spaces exist in postcolonial literature?[8] And if so, what connections exist between postcolonial theories and transculturality?

After my discussion of Creole theories and their implications for women, I examine Welsch's proposed transculturality through discussion of texts, spanning cultures and continents. The works of Simone Schwarz-Bart and Gisèle Pineau are culturally diverse insofar as their examination of women with a history of displacement and no language of origin. Schwarz-Bart's *Un plat de porc aux bananes vertes* and *Pluie et vent sur Télumée Miracle* touch on many of the questions later discussed by the founders of Creole theories, including the historical legacy left by slavery and colonization. These issues are pertinent to representation of the mother since they determine, in part, the role she plays in society and thus how she is perceived by her family. For Pineau, raised both in France and Guadeloupe, migration and exile are central concerns. In *L'espérance-macadam* she sheds light not only on exile as it is experienced by mother figures but also on the physical abuse endured by many women in the French Caribbean. Both authors provide a range of maternal portraits, including grandmothers who fill in for absent or otherwise occupied mothers, mothers who raise their families in exile, adoptive mothers, and mothers who suffer from abuse and abandonment. Schwarz-Bart and Pineau deal directly and indirectly with these controversial issues, exposing some of the potentially troublesome aspects of transculturality.

North Africa is another fertile ground for literary production, documenting encounters that occur between people of different religions, ethnicities, and social groups. Assia Djebar and Malika Mokeddem, much like Schwarz-Bart and Pineau, represent different generations of writers. Djebar's writing can be considered transcultural in that she provides a critique of patriarchal tradition in both Western and North African contexts. She also deconstructs the monolithic image of the Maghreb by revealing divisions within the Muslim culture and by calling attention to the different languages spoken in the region, including Berber and Arabic dialects. In *La Femme sans sépulture*, Djebar provides a mother's account of Algeria's war of liberation through that mother's spectral voice. The novel represents an effort to *reclaim* and *proclaim* the role women played in the war against France. Mokeddem, a medical doctor in the south of France, has published several novels dealing with the struggles of Algerian women both in Algeria and abroad. She also critiques patriarchal tradition in her novels and portrays characters who are influenced by both Muslim and Western traditions as they travel between France and Algeria. *Des rêves et des assassins* recounts a young woman's quest for knowledge about the mother she never knew. Djebar's and Mokeddem's novels both provide examples of mothers who are absent due to death under violent circumstances, revealing the long-lasting reverberations of violence against women in Algerian society. Although both mothers die violent deaths, the children they leave behind nonetheless experience their mothers' absences differently.

Since the Second World War, Quebec's immigrant population has grown, changing the social fabric of the province and diversifying its literary production. Much of Quebec's contemporary literature is thus classified as *littérature migrante*, or migrant literature, reflecting migratory waves and Quebec's changing demographics. Ying Chen, born and raised in China, and Abla Farhoud, a writer of Lebanese descent, are two authors whose works belong to Canada's body of *littérature migrante*. Chen produces work that is inherently transcultural. Her literary creations allude to both the history and traditions of her native China and the fast-changing, globalized society that currently characterizes her homeland. Chen's *L'Ingratitude* chronicles a young woman's suicide and her anger with her spiteful mother. In *Le Bonheur a la queue glissante*, Farhoud gives a voice to Dounia, an illiterate immigrant mother who prepares for her death and who speaks by mediation of her daughter. Although Chen and Farhoud present contrasting mother figures that approach their children differently, both are victims of patriarchal authority, hindered in life and relationships by a system that seeks to repress women.

Before entering deeper into our analysis of diversity and how it impacts women in Francophone postcolonial contexts, we must first discuss the notion of literature as a potential space of resistance. Since the publication of Edward Said's *Orientalism* in 1978, postcolonial theorists have debated the ways in which repressed peoples express themselves, or if in fact they have any agency at all. Gayatri Spivak's seminal essay "Can the Subaltern Speak?" claims that the colonized subject cannot adequately express him- or herself due to the lasting effects of colonial historiography. His or her "voice" is formed within the theoretical framework of colonialism, as the subaltern knows only the oppressor's version of history. The history of the subaltern, both personal and collective, is thus colored by colonialism. This, according to Spivak, is that which the subaltern *cannot* speak. Homi Bhabha has a different take on the power of the dominated person to express him- or herself. He claims that colonialism is a complex phenomenon that can foster cultural hybridity, creating a "Third Space" of enunciation in which the oppressed person seeks and obtains the power to speak out against his or her oppressor (34–35). Yet the question that remains is *can* and *how* does literature offer a third space, that is to say, a space of resistance in which the Other can inscribe his or her voice? Consideration of literature as a possible Third Space impacts my study of mothers and daughters depicted in literature, as it attracts attention to discourses that situate themselves in opposition to the repressive forces of patriarchal systems. How do authors choose to transmit the voices of marginalized women? In what contexts are daughters inspired to weave their mothers' stories? In what ways do absent mothers and daughters continue to impact the families they leave behind, and what commentaries do they make on their respective patriarchal societies? Stemming from these fundamental questions, the present study moves beyond debates on the "Third Space" and the subaltern to examine how postcolonial literature can rewrite history and question the status of historical discourse as an objective one.[9]

GLISSANT AND COMPANY: ARTICULATING CREOLE IDENTITIES

When readers engage with a literary text, they often gain understanding of themselves or others. In this sense, fiction provides a space in which readers encounter, ponder, and perhaps begin to disentangle long-held perceptions. In the 1980s, intellectuals from Martinique, including Edouard Glissant, Jean Bernabé, Patrick Chamoiseau, and Raphaël Confiant, began to use literature as a means to address questions unique to black West Indians. Their works grapple with problems of language, the erasing of group history, and matters of acculturation, deportation, and diaspora. They strive to develop the concept of an identity specific to their islands rather than project a more general image of black people as their predecessors had done in the Negritude movement. Most prominent among them is Glissant, who progressively breaks with the concept of a pure black identity, promoting *métissage*[10] and diversity in *Le Discours antillais* (1981). In *Introduction à une Poétique du divers* (1996), he expounds on his understanding of identity through interpretation of Gilles Deleuze and Félix Guattari's theory of rhizomatic identity:

> Il ne s'agit pas de se déraciner, il s'agit de concevoir la racine moins intolérante, moins sectaire: une identité-racine qui ne tue pas autour d'elle mais qui au contraire étend ses branches vers les autres. Ce que d'après Deleuze et Guattari j'appelle une identité-rhizome. (132)

> [It is not a matter of uprooting oneself; it involves conceiving of the least intolerant root, the least sectarian: a root identity that doesn't kill that which surrounds it but to the contrary spreads its branches towards others. This is what I call, in the vein of Deleuze and Guattari, a rhizome identity.][11]

While Deleuze and Guattari perceive the *identité-rhizome* as essential to the moment in which one "becomes different" (Stagoll 21–22), Glissant's interpretation of the idea is that one's identity is in constant evolution and mutation.[12] Rather than eventually achieving an ultimate, definitive identity, one possesses an ever-changing identity that transforms with the passage of time and experience.

Glissant's *Poétique de la Relation* (1990) is key in understanding the development of Creole ideas and essential to the present study's consideration of contemporary identities. While his early work focuses on the author's perception of Martinique as a nation, his later work advocates an infinite, placeless creolization, "a rather more far-reaching incorporation, into the univocity of a new world order based on nothing other than internal metamorphosis, dislocation and exchange" (Hallward 442). So

Glissant shifts his focus from his own island to the world itself. The importance of a sense of place is eventually minimized, while the value of wandering, or nomandism, is emphasized. He distinguishes, for instance, between two types of identity: *l'identité-racine* (root identity) and *l'identité-relation* (relational identity). The former is molded by tradition, territory, and myths of origins. The latter is shaped by experience, contact between cultures, and wandering.

Glissant's *Poétique* throws weighty questions out for discussion. What is identity? How does one form his or her own identity? How does a group identity differ from personal identity? What is the significance of "relation," or shared knowledge, in the formation of these identities? Glissant also leaves some significant questions unanswered. He fails to account for evolving postcolonial identities that are linked to place, change of place, diasporas, and the passage of time. For instance, he does not reflect on the case of a person from the French Caribbean living in the metropolis. Far from his or her island, that person's identity evolves differently from that of a compatriot who has not left the island. An inevitable meeting of cultures occurs in the life of a displaced person, and as Glissant has indicated, these meetings are an important element of creolization. Yet leading life at such a distance from one's homeland creates lacunas in collective experience, as is evidenced by Mariotte's experience in *Un plat de porc*. Her cultural encounters prove to be neither enriching nor fulfilling, as she is not only far from her native land but also completely cut off from the traditions and experiences she associates with her island. As we see in the case of Mariotte, the longer she spends away from her homeland, the more emotionally wrenching it is for her to recall and identify with her island childhood. Recalling a seemingly distant past—both geographically and temporally defined—becomes more and more painful as time passes.

Just as one's identity is linked to a specific place, so too can it be linked to the concept of difference. That is to say, a person is oftentimes attached to that which distinguishes him from others, as it is those traits that make him unique. In *Poétique de la Relation* Glissant explains that claiming to understand differences can actually distort the identity of another: "Je 'comprends' ta différence, c'est-à-dire que je la mets en rapport, sans hiérarchiser, avec ma norme. Je t'admets à existence, dans mon système. Je te crée une nouvelle fois" (204). [I "understand" your difference, that's to say that I compare it to my norm without placing it in a hierarchy. I acknowledge your existence, in my system. I create you again.] In *Un plat de porc*, Mariotte seems to have come to terms with the fact that she cannot articulate her experiences to the white people in the home, so when they interact with her, she regales them with silly tales "qui plaisent aux Européens" (162). [that please Europeans.] Yet one day as they are making their way up the stairwell, Jeanne asks for a *real* story about Mariotte's childhood, and Mariotte hesitates: "Elle savait, va . . . qu'elle devinait . . . pourquoi ça m'était impossible . . . qu'elle les sub-odorait, tous ces mondes qu'il y avait entre nous et que ça ne pouvait pas se franchir par des paroles!" (PP 162–163). [She knew, you see . . . that she guessed . . . why that was impossible for me . . . that she sensed them, all these worlds that there were between us and that words couldn't over-come.] In this passage, the Schwarz-Barts seem to perceive the concept of difference that Glissant would elucidate some twenty years later. As the elderly women slowly make their way up the stairs, Mariotte attunes the reader to her and Jeanne's shared understanding that Mariotte's persona in the care facility does not authentically represent her experience, due to "all these worlds" that exist between her and the other residents. This simplified, flat persona allows the residents to contemplate her on their terms—with the racist, sexist, and classist undertones that make her pres-ence an unthreatening one.

The result of the fabricated identity, perpetuated in part by Mariotte, fosters a false and shallow perception of her life. Glissant, too, realizes the existence of untrue and potentially harmful perceptions. In that vein, he proposes that we not only support the right to difference but also the right to *l'opacité*, or opaqueness. The notion of opaqueness refers to a person's unique traits that distinguish him or her from others and which *cannot be wholly understood by others*. Glissant encourages a harmoni-ous coexistence of opaque beings who are aware of differences but who make no effort to alter others' unique, sometimes incomprehensible char-acteristics:

> Non pas seulement consentir au droit à la différence mais, plus avant, au droit à l'opacité, qui n'est pas l'enfermement dans une autarcie impénétrable, mais la subsistance dans une singularité non réductible. Des opacités peuvent coexister, confluer, tramant des tissus dont la véritable compréhension porterait sur la texture de cette trame et non pas sur la nature des composantes. (*Poétique* 204)

[Not only consent to the right to difference but, more profoundly, to
the right to opacity, which is not imprisonment in an impenetrable
autarky, but subsistence in an irreducible singularity. Opacities can
coexist, converge, weaving fabrics of which the true comprehension
would be linked to the texture of this weave and not the nature of its
components.]

L'opacité thus incarnates the synthesis of characteristics and experiences
that differentiate an individual from others as well as *that which remains
incomprehensible* to others. In Glissant's optimistic mode of thinking,
interpersonal exchange is enriched because there are certain elements that
people do not understand about one another.

How does l'opacité relate to Glissant's view of creolization, and how
can the two be applied to contemporary postcolonial realities? Does one's
right to difference and his or her consequent opaqueness compromise the
creolization so dear to Glissant? Would an extensive process of creolization over a number of generations minimize or eliminate l'opacité that
Glissant claims we each possess, therefore creating a uniform society?
Glissant provides little insight concerning the dynamic between l'opacité
and creolization, but it is useful to apply the two ideas to contemporary
postcolonial societies. Glissant discusses a variety of regions affected by
colonization at one time or another, including the Caribbean, Brazil, Ar-
gentina, Mexico, and even the United States, the South in particular. Yet
he does not underscore the fundamental differences and nuances between
their colonial pasts, which ultimately lead to different degrees of métissage as well as inherent differences in both group and personal identity.

This study alone provides multiple examples of people whose lives
evolve differently according to the circumstances of their postcolonial
experience. For Dounia, the protagonist in Farhoud's *Le bonheur a la
queue glissante*, assimilation is out of the question after multiple moves
and never having learned to read and write. She focuses on communication at a basic level, using broken French and vivid gestures as she plays
with her Canadian grandchildren or talks with her landlady. Chen's
L'Ingratitude depicts Yan-Zi, a young career woman who feels exiled
from her own parents due to her refusal to abide by traditional Chinese
familial expectations. Unfortunately, she also feels like an outcast from
Western society, so her experience of métissage is neither affirming nor
fruitful. In *La Femme sans sépulture*, Djebar shares the story of Zoulikha,
who is a stranger in her own country due to her insistence upon personal

freedom—speaking her mind in public puts her in grave danger, but she persists. Each of these women experiences different degrees of belonging or rejection by their culture of origin or host culture. Their bumpy processes of creolization, or better, transformation, contribute to the opaqueness, or intrinsic and very personal differences, described by Glissant. Do creolization and rhizomatic identity encompass the various colonial histories we know and study today? More specifically, how might mother figures negotiate identity formation in a dynamic world of meetings, interactions, and transformations?

CREOLE *AVANT LA LETTRE*

Since Bernabé, Chamoiseau, and Confiant published the Creole manifesto *Eloge de la Créolité* in 1989, countless studies have documented the complexities of Creole literature, including the questions of bilingualism, the history of slavery, and identity issues linked to these matters.[13] Interestingly enough, none of the theorists of Creoleness addresses Creoleness in reference to gender and how it *is* or *could be* experienced by women. The place of women's voices in history as well as the roles mothers play in the construction of Creole identities comprise a feminine version of Creoleness that remains a field still largely unexplored.

The two Creole manifestos and Glissant's *Poétique de la Relation* are revolutionary works that have helped to bring attention to the literatures of the French Caribbean. Yet is there recognition of Creole feminine literary creation in *Poétique de la Relation* and *L'Eloge*? Are these theories useful in examination of the works of women writers from the French Caribbean and elsewhere? It is interesting to note that although the Creole theories were elaborated by male intellectuals from Martinique and the authors they quote are male, several of the best-known novels from the region are written by *women* from *Guadeloupe*. We can turn to examples from Maryse Condé, Simone Schwarz-Bart, Gisèle Pineau, and Myriam Warner-Vieyra. Each of these women portrays a unique facet of Creoleness as experienced by women. None of these authors subscribes specifically to a vision of Creoleness proclaimed by their male counterparts. Rather, they illustrate the diversity of Creoleness through description of tradition, incorporation of French and local proverbs, subversion of language, and portrayal of the different experiences of each protagonist.

Whereas Schwarz-Bart's *Pluie et vent sur Télumée Miracle* (1972) tells the story of a young girl growing up in a Guadeloupian village and influenced by the Creole stories and proverbs shared by her grandmother, Pineau reveals the diasporic experiences of both girls and mature women in *Un Papillon dans la cité* (1992) and *L'Exil selon Julia* (1996). In *Juletane* (1982), Warner-Vieyra recounts the stark isolation and cultural difficulties experienced by an Antillean woman living abroad, and in *La Belle Créole* (2001), Condé examines the seemingly endless métissage experienced by her characters who live in all corners of the earth. Subsequently, these Creole writers depict different diasporas, both colonial and postcolonial.

The various Creole experiences presented by these women writers are not addressed by Glissant, Bernabé, Chamoiseau, and Confiant. Although *Lettres créoles* devotes a number of pages to contemporary Caribbean writers, including Schwarz-Bart and Condé, no issues specifically pertaining to women are addressed. Rather, the authors describe Condé as an author that "shatters" the African mirror (Chamoiseau and Confiant 204) and Schwarz-Bart as one who communicates the richness of Creoleness without putting forth a political agenda (Chamoiseau and Confiant 247–249). As A. James Arnold remarks in his article "The Gendering of Créolité," these prominent Creole thinkers neglect to mention the elderly Creole women who are "repositories of oral history, folk medicine, and stories of all sorts" (30). While Chamoiseau and Confiant celebrate the *conteur créole* and his respected position on the plantation, they do not document the roles that women played and continue to play in inspiring literary creation in the French Caribbean.

Un plat de porc is one of many novels that illustrates the essential feminine tile that is missing from the colorful mosaic of Creoleness. Mariotte's imagined returns to her village are dominated by women: her dying grandmother, who is always at the heart of the story, and her solicitous mother and aunt, who anxiously attend to her. In her hazy and troubling homecoming, she observes the preparations leading up to the death of Man Louise—the solemn vigil by the dying woman's bedside, the preparation of the last meal, and the visit of the Creole medicine man. Mariotte's mother and aunt are instrumental in the organization of their mother's last hours on Earth, and the rituals surrounding their mother's passing would not be carried out if it weren't for their desire to respect the cultural traditions surrounding death.

Although several Creole thinkers seem to have neglected or ignored the existence of Creoleness as lived and described by women, Maryse Condé has long been aware of the various roles women fill in the French Caribbean and the larger Francophone world. In fact, even before publication of the Creole manifestos, Condé wrote about the place of women in the French West Indies. In *La parole des femmes* (1979), she analyzes the feminine side of French Caribbean literature, drawing attention to subjects concerning women writers and their characters, such as the manner in which power relations are negotiated between men and women. This work is critical because it is the first to examine Caribbean literature in French in as far as it concerns women and women writers: "Nous avons pensé qu'il serait intéressant d'interroger quelques écrivains femmes des Caraïbes francophones pour cerner l'image qu'elles ont d'elles-mêmes et appréhender les problèmes dont elles souffrent éventuellement" (Condé, *La parole*, 5). [We thought that it would be interesting to question some women writers from the Francophone Caribbean in order to determine the image that they have of themselves and to comprehend the problems from which they might suffer.] She discusses topics such as the education of young girls and women's relationships with the men in their lives, including fathers, boyfriends, and husbands. In the years since the publication of *La parole des femmes*, Condé has elaborated on her original propos, accounting for societal changes occurring in subsequent decades. It is worthwhile to consider the trajectory of her thought alongside other critics, as it demonstrates Condé's singular place as a postcolonial theorist.

In addition to voicing women's perspectives on maternity and the education of girls, *La parole* also contemplates the role of men in the French Caribbean: "Frustré, dépossédé, l'Antillais s'est réfugié dans des attitudes d'irresponsabilité qui ont survécu à l'évolution politique des Iles" (Condé 36). [Frustrated, deprived of land and property, the Antillean man has sought refuge in the attitudes of irresponsibility that survived the political evolution of the Islands]. Condé then asserts that male irresponsibility in the Caribbean must be put in socio-economic perspective (*La parole* 36). Yet in a 2001 interview with Bonnie Thomas, Condé acknowledges the evolution of gender relations in the Caribbean since the publication of *La parole*. For instance, Condé expresses her desire that scholars and authors go beyond the traditional images of the Caribbean man: "For example, there's a young couple renting a house behind mine.

I can see that the image of the man is changing. He takes on a lot of responsibility, he shares his time and the work, and so we mustn't any longer talk about the sort of man who doesn't lift a finger" (Thomas 170). She also cites the example of women and men who work together in the fight for Guadeloupian independence (Thomas 170). It is obvious that Condé perceives a need to surpass *La parole des femmes* so as to account for the evolution of societies, yet she maintains certain tenets of the work: "Yes, there still exists a sort of tolerance toward masculine excesses. Women have a sort of belief that men are always men and you can't change them" (Thomas 171). In reading Thomas's interview with Condé, we can see that the writer is acutely aware of identities that evolve with the passage of time and changes in society.

Even in accounting for societal changes that occur over the decades, the social and historical context of family life in the French Caribbean still places women at the center of the family unit. In *La parole*, Condé demonstrates that the absence of men, whether they are husbands, boyfriends, or fathers, makes for women who play multiple roles within the family, including breadwinner, parent, cook, and housekeeper. Contemporary Creole literature written by women not only acknowledges the realities faced by single mothers but also calls attention to the stratification of social classes in the French Caribbean, which leaves most of these mothers at the bottom.

In addition to explaining why the woman is at the heart of the family unit, *La parole* examines a woman's complex, oftentimes complicated role in society as a single mother, a grandmother raising her grandchildren, or as a woman who chooses not to marry and have children. Another issue raised by Condé in the work is that of religious practices, including the intermixing of witchcraft and Roman Catholic traditions. She explains that references to the traditions of witchcraft, black magic, and white magic can represent the importance of such practices in contemporary Caribbean society (Condé, *La parole*, 53).

Pierre Bourdieu's view of witchcraft is different than that of Condé's. While Condé emphasizes the use of witchcraft by female protagonists as representative of cultural practices carried over from African ancestors and resistance against the colonizer's imposed religion, he groups use of magic by women with other forms of "soft violence," including lies and sexual passivity. He writes that soft violence provides women with a way to retaliate against physical and non-physical violence imposed by a pa-

triarchal society (Bourdieu 32). Both Condé's and Bourdieu's explanations regarding magic relate to Mariotte's interactions in *Un plat de porc*.
Although she never makes her reader aware of an occasion in which she
employs magic to influence others, she does refer to the fear that her
supposed spells inspires in her peers (PP 35). She never seems to refute
any stereotype that others make about Africa or the Caribbean, and so
references to magic or life in the tropics come to symbolize her "exotic"
background. Yet Bourdieu's analysis of magic also pertains to this protagonist, as the simple threat of witchcraft provides the oppressed older
woman with the possibility of negotiating and acquiring power, as these
misunderstood practices incite fear in her French companions. [14]

In daring to address taboo subjects—abandonment, single parenthood,
and magic—Condé in effect normalizes discourse on the sensitive subjects that touch the lives of women and that appear as themes in literature
written by women. Through her analysis of various works written by
women, she sheds light on a sort of "feminine" Creoleness that the Creole
manifestos will neglect—one that takes into account the significant role
of women in a given culture, which can be any combination of teacher,
healer, or mother. *La parole* is thus the foundational work of Condé's
theory, which will also serve to influence critics of later generations.

FOLLOWING IN CONDÉ'S FOOTSTEPS:
FURTHER EXAMINATION OF WOMEN'S VOICES

In subsequent decades, other critics have built on Condé's work, writing
on aspects of Creoleness as presented by women authors. Lydie Moudileno's *L'écrivain antillais au miroir de sa littérature* (1997) examines the
roles of women writers and characters in several novels by authors from
Martinique and Guadeloupe. She observes that women's writing is a
"process of creolization" due to its inclusion of writing, oral tradition,
imagination, and the symbolic (Moudileno 30).

She calls to mind the diverse contributions of women writers to the
body of Creole literature, including recognition of a woman's essential
place in society as repository of collective memory. She thus specifies the
nature of "feminine" Creoleness expressed through literary creation.

Furthermore, Moudileno notes the absence of patriarchal references in
Schwarz-Bart and Condé's novels, referring to a *détournement*, or turning

away, "qui met à profit l'espace du livre pour ménager la possibilité d'une parole oubliée, éclipsée par les discours successifs de la colonisation et de la négritude" (36). [that uses the space of the book to make room for the possibility of a forgotten voice eclipsed by the successive discourses of colonization and Negritude.] Moudileno suggests that in moving away from patriarchal discourse, women writers of the Caribbean offer another path to understanding the Creoleness that defines the French Caribbean. Rather than contradict their male contemporaries, the women authors provide a complementary perspective that serves to give a more complete image of the region, its traditions, and its people. In addition, the forgotten *parole*, or voice, that Moudileno evokes acts as a subtle intertext to the work of her predecessor. In her *La parole*, Condé had begun to expose the condition of Antillean women as portrayed in literature. Likewise, Moudileno asserts literature as a method to unearth or expose women's forgotten voices. As Moudileno demonstrates, this proposed "feminine" Creoleness creates a literary space enabling writers to express and explore a universe whose survival is assured by women. While not condoning or criticizing the French Caribbean's important male figures—such as Aimé Césaire—Condé, Schwarz-Bart, and younger generations of writers use the literary space to weave stories neglected by the writers of history.

Bonnie Thomas's 2006 book *Breadfruit or Chestnut?* provides an insightful look at the function of gender in literature of the French Caribbean more than twenty years after the publication of *La parole des femmes*. Directly alluding to Condé's book in the title and first chapter of her study, Thomas attests to the influence of Condé's work on her own as well as its pertinence in contemporary society. Through examination of contemporary novels, her work analyzes the gendered identities of the "past saturated societies" of Martinique and Guadeloupe (Thomas 1). Whereas Condé's focus is solely on women writers, Thomas draws comparisons between the French Caribbean's most prominent authors, both women and men. She labels the novels of Glissant, Chamoiseau and Confiant as "fiction largely based on the past" and that of women as based in the present or looking to the future (Thomas 153). In fact, her book aims to surpass the generalizations made by other postcolonial critics concerning gender relations that do not hold true in contemporary Caribbean societies, including those of Condé's *La parole*. Thomas thus advances the study of Creoleness in a feminine context by problematizing gender relations as they are represented in literature by authors of both sexes, breaking away from the dichotomy of the strong woman and the weak man so often present in Francophone literature.

BEYOND THE CARIBBEAN

Although Maryse Condé is most readily associated with the French Caribbean, in large part thanks to her impressive body of literary work, her theoretical interests extend well beyond the Americas. Like her colleague Edouard Glissant, she surpasses geographical categorization, perceiving connections between writers from diverse cultural backgrounds. In her 2011 preface to Eric Touya de Marenne's book *Francophone Women Writers*, Condé lays out the complexities of the study of women's writing:

> In their majority, women write about the world as they experience—a world too often characterized by exclusion, intolerance, lack of consideration and recognition. Some, on the contrary, turn their backs on reality and become real magicians. Through their art of story-telling, they dream up a new planet where irrespective of gender, skin color, creed or origin, every individual communicates with each other. (x)

Condé's analysis points to commonalities that lend themselves to rich discussions on societal structures, inequality, tradition, and modernity. A Creoleness including the feminine includes these points of intersection—*exclusion, intolerance, lack of consideration*, and *recognition*. Yet these aspects of women's lives are in no way limited to the French West Indies.

As evidenced in *Poétique de la Relation*, creolization is intended to encompass multiple regions in which cultural métissage has taken place or in which meetings between cultures could potentially occur, creating a unique dynamic conveyed by and through literature. Thus, virtually any postcolonial area could be considered "Creole," including North Africa, Asia, and Canada. The term "Creoleness" is, however, problematic, as it is inextricably linked to the French Caribbean in the minds of most readers. Given the fact that the present work discusses literature from multiple regions—the French Caribbean, Algeria, and Canada—I find it useful to employ a term that encompasses the geographically diverse nature of the work. To that end, Wolfgang Welsch's theory of transculturality accounts

for the extensive contact between members of different cultures throughout the world. In conjunction with one another, Creoleness and transculturality allow for a dynamic analysis of literary works from Francophone
postcolonial regions.

AN UNHAPPY TRANSCULTURALITY?

As time passes, groups' perceptions of themselves and their histories
transform. Thus, concepts of culture evolve with the people who make up
a given society. In his chapter "Transculturality—the Puzzling Form of
Cultures Today," Welsch outlines the ways in which people have defined
culture since the eighteenth century. His discussion includes the notions
of singular cultures, interculturality, and the American concept of multiculturalism. Welsch points out that each successive theory develops a
greater awareness of and interaction with others. For example, interculturality seeks to promote understanding between cultures as they interact
with one another.[15] Present-day Europe exemplifies interculturality, as
members of the European Union strive to maintain specific national identities all while respecting the laws imposed by the organization.[16] Multiculturalism incarnates many of the same goals of interculturality. Multiculturalism was first meant to call attention to the economic hardships of
ethnic minorities, such as African Americans. Yet according to Karnoouh, it came to represent a broader group of individuals within
American society: "It now includes groups which, after successful economic integration, continue to flaunt their cultural difference. Now multiculturalism refers to a sort of equalization of all differences, whatever the
source" (129).[17] Karnoouh refers to a "homogenization of values" of
minority groups, including Native Americans, African Americans, and
Hispanics.

It is clear that interculturality and multiculturalism both account for
interactions between diverse peoples that occur with increased travel and
communication. Yet Welsch asserts that although both seek tolerance and
understanding, they underscore the boundaries between groups, maintaining the premise that cultures are spheres ("Transculturality" 21–22).
Finding that interculturality and multiculturality do not adequately respond to the conditions of today's world, Welsch proposes transculturality as an appropriate means to articulate contemporary cultures. He

claims that the high degree of intertwinement in modern societies calls for a new vision and understanding of the way in which cultures, and therefore people, relate to one another: "The new forms of entanglement are a consequence of migratory processes, as well as of worldwide material and immaterial communications systems and economic interdependencies" (Welsch, "Transculturality" 23). The entanglements to which Welsch refers make for hybrid cultures in which identities form through exposure to numerous cultural factors that are all present in the same society. He thus defines transculturality as follows: "The concept of transculturality aims for a multi-meshed and inclusive, not separatist and exclusive understanding of culture. It intends a culture and society whose pragmatic feats exist not in delimitation, but in the ability to link and undergo transition" (Welsch, "Transculturality" 26).[18] Transculturality differs from multiculturality and interculturality in that the barriers that have been articulated in preceding cultural models no longer function as obstacles. Welsch sees cultural components as cutting through these boundaries, creating new personal identities not linked to the nation.

Although transculturality is not intended as a literary or cultural movement, Welsch's view of culture intersects with many of the fundamental ideas that Creoleness promotes.[19] Transculturality names a phenomenon that exists in Western and non-Western cultures throughout the world—that of cultures meeting, co-existing, and very often influencing one another. As previously noted, Creoleness, which is at the same time literary and political, not only recognizes but *encourages* mutual influence between cultures. Seeing as how both concepts promote the meeting and blending of cultures, one might wonder if cultural uniformity is a risk. Welsch believes that one must reconsider diversity in order to understand its transcultural character:

> Under conditions of transculturality diversity doesn't disappear altogether, rather its mode is altered. [. . .] Diversity in the traditional mode of single cultures does in fact disappear. Instead, a new type of diversity is formed: the diversity of different ways of life with a transcultural cut. It too is distinguished by a high degree of individualization and manifold differences—at least as high as attested to for single cultures by the traditional conception. ("Transculturality" 28)

Thus, a transcultural society, or better, a transcultural individual, undergoes transition without the risk of becoming identical to his or her peers.

Difference is not defined by national or ethnic affiliation but rather through interactions on an individual level. Each person's "transcultural blend" or "transcultural cut" is unique, as each person's identity is formed through diverse experiences.

Although he insists on diversity, in a 2012 chapter, Welsch extends his original theory by underlining the commonalities of cultures:

> If there were no common basis to cultures at all, then the fact that we can transfer semantic items (beliefs, thoughts, perceptions, yearnings, etc.) from one culture to another and integrate them into a context which originally was not theirs would be completely unintelligible. ("Commonalities" 12)

Much as Condé underlines the experiences of exclusion and intolerance shared by women, Welsch acknowledges the inherent bridges that exist between cultures. He thus establishes transculturality as a cultural theory unbound by time and space. To illustrate his argument of commonalities, he asks why people can be moved by a work of art from a foreign culture, then explains that "Though not made for us, the works seem to address us; we feel attracted to them, fascinated by them. They appear to bear a promise or a challenge to which we respond" (Welsch, "Commonalities" 13). Although we do not experience them in their original context and likely not as the creator intended, works of art or literature from other times and places nonetheless move us. Thus, according to Welsch, "we experience them as transculturally effective" ("Commonalities" 13).

Lamberto Tassinari's remarks on the term "transcultural" echo the unfixed nature of transculturality highlighted by Welsch:

> Ce mot implique la traversée d'une seule culture en même temps que son dépassement. L'unité qu'il sous-tend n'a pas la même résonance que celle qu'évoquent les termes "inter-culturel" ou "multiculturel." Ceux-ci définissent un ensemble et le circonscrivent dans un espace et un temps, alors que le transculturel ne possède pas de périmètre. (Qtd. in Moisan 288–289).

> [This word implies the simultaneous crossing and surpassing of a single culture. The unity that it underpins does not have the same resonance of the terms "inter-cultural" or "multicultural." These define a grouping and circumscribe it in a space and time, while the transcultural possesses no perimeter.]

Tassinari projects an image of a limitless number of possible cultural encounters and passages due to the absence of prescribed boundaries. Yet he also points out the lack of unity that exists in such a model. The cultural passages he references recall Glissant's notion of relational identity, formed through wandering and contact. Interplay between transculturality and Creole theories is natural, given the number of concerns they share regarding the formation of identities in a world where contact between individuals of different backgrounds occurs on a regular basis.

Due to the numerous intersections of the two theories, the present work employs the term "transculturality" when referring to notions incarnated by Creoleness. Although Welsch makes literary references in his article on transculturality, he does not present the theory as one that is primarily literary.[20] Nonetheless, in his book *Une histoire de l'écriture migrante au Québec*, Clément Moisan characterizes recent Quebecois literature as "transcultural," taking into account the ethnic transformation of Quebec's population in the last seventy years: "Le transculturel, caractéristique de la présente période, dépasse la mise en présence ou en conflit des cultures pour dégager des passages entre elles et dessiner leur traversée respective" (207). [The transcultural, characteristic of the present period, surpasses the clash of cultures to open passages between them and delineate their respective crossing.]

In addition, in recent years a number of critics have employed the theory of transculturality in the study of world literature in English. Among those are *Transcultural English Studies: Theories, Fictions, Realities* and *Literature for Our Times: Postcolonial Studies in the Twenty-First Century*, published in 2009 and 2012 respectively. The two collections serve to anchor transculturality in literary studies. Much as English departments led the way in postcolonial studies, these initial studies on literature in transcultural contexts may prove integral to the implementation of transcultural theories across the disciplines.

The present work employs the term "transcultural" in reference to the construction of mother and daughter figures in the works of the selected authors. Transculturality in a feminine context builds on Condé's *Parole des femmes*, addressing questions pertinent to women in contemporary French-speaking societies, such as her rights in a given society and her role in the transmission of culture. Of utmost importance and the focus of the present study is the role of the woman in the family unit and her interaction with her family members, given the specific circumstances of her postcolonial existence. Other important issues include the perception of women in the greater community; the role of language, whether it be her own or that of the oppressor; a woman's place in the postcolonial landscape; and her participation in the formation of her society.

Consideration of the positions women hold in different postcolonial, French-speaking contexts will reveal the struggle and unhappiness that are not necessarily accounted for in Welsch's vision of transculturality. While he describes the theory as "multi-meshed and inclusive" (Welsch, "Transculturality" 26), the present work examines characters who often fall through the cracks of tranculturality's inclusive intentions. In her chapter "The Missing Link," Sissy Helff identifies refugees and illegal migrants as groups that do not easily fit into the paradigm of transculturality due to their unstable living situations and the difficulty in accounting for them in the bureaucracy (198). To her list of liminal peoples, I would add the women, many of them migrants, whose cultural contacts often prove to be painful, shameful, and frustrating. Their "transcultural blend," while formative and fundamental to their development, makes for an unhappy transculturality not accounted for in Welsch's theory.

Spaces of Creation opens a discussion on the development and transmission of women's voices in challenging transcultural contexts. As women move through cultures, sometimes unwillingly, how do they link, transition, and ultimately transform? Upon first glance, their confined situations may appear stagnant and lackluster. Yet the limitations imposed by their transcultural entanglements—marginalization, silence, and separation from loved ones—fuel self-examination and consequently, self-expression. The present study creates links between feminine literary figures grounded in different cultural traditions, bringing to light the creative connections that exist between them. Consequently, it invites us to reexamine mother-daughter interactions from a broader, transcultural perspective.

Chapter 2 of this study examines the development of mothers and daughters in their specific transcultural situations. The chapter reveals important parallels between works from across the Francophone world concerning the ways in which women operate in their culturally diverse communities. Each of the seven novels treated in this study documents traumatic situations brought on by displacement or violence. Consequently, the characters experience different degrees of cultural entwinement ranging from enriching interactions to virtually no contact with people outside the family. In *La Femme sans sépulture* by Assia Djebar, *Des rêves et des assassins* by Malika Mokkedem, and *L'Ingratitude* by Ying Chen, young adult women strive to move through life without maternal guidance, leaving them feeling untethered and marginal. In Simone Schwarz-Bart's *Pluie et vent* and *Un plat de porc*, women from the French Caribbean face prejudice and sexism in their encounters with Europeans, demonstrating how these troubling relationships have influenced their family dynamics. Finally, the protagonists of *L'espérance-macadam* by Gisèle Pineau and *Le Bonheur a la queue glissante* by Abla Farhoud both crave the comfort of silence as an escape from the chaos that awaits them in their families and communities. Each of these works sheds light on the complex, even painful nature of inevitable transcultural meetings.

Chapter 3 examines the representation of various spaces that spark contemplation and creation on the part of women. Given the geographic diversity of the works discussed in this study, we are presented with diverse spaces that serve to inspire reflection and subsequent self-expression—rural landscapes, cityscapes, and quiet, mental spaces. In *Pluie et vent* and *L'espérance-macadam*, mothers and daughters are correlated with the natural world, which can be either affirming or heart-wrenching. In *Un plat de porc* and *Le Bonheur a la queue glissante*, characters evolve in an urban setting, far away from their rural roots. Consequently, they seek refuge in journaling or inner dialogue. Also in a cosmopolitan environment, the protagonist in *L'Ingratitude* finds that she is unable to connect with others—family, boyfriends, and co-workers included. She chooses to escape from her impersonal and anonymous life through suicide, then proceeds to drift in an undefined post-life dimension devoid of happiness. The physical and mental spaces these women inhabit stir up traumatic experiences from past and present. Nonetheless, the chapter will demonstrate that they serve as valuable spaces of creation that help to voice the struggles that arise in transcultural contexts.

The final chapter explores the ongoing relationship between the living and the dead in three novels: *La Femme sans sépulture*, *L'Ingratitude*, and *Des rêves et des assassins*. With varying degrees of frustration, the spectral narrators in *La Femme sans sépulture* and *L'Ingratitude* attempt to communicate after death, rehashing their life stories and seeking perspective and understanding. The protagonist in *Des rêves et des assassins* also sets out on a quest of understanding. Never having known the circumstances surrounding her mother's disappearance and death, she leaves Algeria to seek answers in France, where her mother spent her last years. In each case, the loneliness brought on by death ends up making way for a space of creation or exchange. Oftentimes tragic, the stories they weave nonetheless exude hope for freedom from the constraints imposed upon many women in culturally diverse societies.

NOTES

1. In Creole, *Man* is a respectful title for an older woman.
2. On March 16, 2007, *Le Monde* published a literary manifesto, *Pour une littérature monde*. Authored by Alain Mabanckou, Jean Rouand, and Michel Le Bris, it was signed by several contemporary authors and proposes abandoning the categorization of literature as *Francophone* in favor of studying it in the context of *world literature*. Debate ensued among authors and scholars, and no consensus has been reached concerning the best terminology. I have elected to use the term *francophone* in this book, as it is less cumbersome than *world literature in French* or *world literature of French expression*.
3. A few works in which mother-daughter relationships evolve in culturally diverse settings include Assia Djebar's *La Femme sans sépulture* and Abla Farhoud's *Le Bonheur a la queue glissante*, both which will be examined in subsequent pages. Several of Gisèle Pineau's novels, including those written for young adults, expose the intricacies of such relationships: *Un Papillon dans la cité*, *L'exil selon Julia*, *Mes quatre femmes*, and *L'espérance-macadam*. Later in the chapter, I will elaborate on these familial relationships and their function in contemporary Francophone literature.
4. Throughout the book, I use the spelling *postcolonial* rather than *post-colonial* according to Ashcroft's distinction: "The hyphen puts an emphasis on the discursive and material effects of the historical 'fact' of colonialism, while the term 'postcolonialism' has come to represent an increasingly indiscriminate attention to cultural difference and marginality of all kinds, whether a consequence of the historical experience of colonialism or not" (23).
5. Hirsch's *The Mother/Daughter Plot* will be treated in chapter 2.
6. See Green's "Simone Schwarz-Bart et la tradition féminine aux Antilles" and Lequin's "The Legacy of Words: Mothers as Agents of Cultural Subterfuge and Subversion."
7. These concerns, discussed in depth in chapter 2, appear elsewhere in world literature. In English, Nigerian Buchi Emecheta's *The Joys of Motherhood* depicts the clash between a traditional society's expectations for family life and

the realities women face in navigating romantic relationships and childbearing. In Spanish, Chilean author Isabel Allende traces the violence and deception endured by three generations of women from the del Valle family in her novel *La casa de los espíritus*.

8. Postcolonial studies were slow to take root in French departments on both sides of the Atlantic, perhaps due in part to resistance of its Anglo-Saxon origins. After the new millennium, however, the tide started to change. Published in 2003, *Francophone Postcolonial Studies: A Critical Introduction*, edited by Charles Forsdick and David Murphy, seeks to place postcolonial studies within a Francophone context. In the introduction, they explain: "One of the ironies of this 'French' reluctance to engage with postcolonial theory is that the postcolonial debate was, in part, launched by anti-colonial French-language writers such as Aimé Césaire, Frantz Fanon, Albert Memmi and Jean-Paul Sartre" (8). Yet the last fifteen years have seen a growing acceptance of postcolonial scholarship in academia, especially outside of France.

9. Other scholars who do such work include Anne Donadey, Françoise Lionnet, Michael Dash, Dominique Fisher, Mireille Rosello, Valérie Orlando, and Typhaine Leservot.

10. Sarah Barbour and Gerise Herndon note that the word *métissage* originally referred to hybridization of plants, but "it has come to mean, briefly, the amalgamation or braiding of diverse cultural components or transculturaltion that creates a new cultural entity or identity" (156).

11. All translations are mine unless otherwise noted.

12. For Deleuze and Guattari, a *devenir*, or "a becoming," represents a moment of métissage. Cliff Stagoll highlights the importance of the act of transformation. He explains: "Rather than a product, final or interim, becoming is the very dynamism of change, situated between heterogenous terms and tending towards no particular goal or end-state" (Stagoll 21–22).

13. The use of Creole was prohibited during colonization and was not put into writing until 1980.

14. For more on religious practices and witchcraft in *Pluie et vent*, see Maria Anagnostopoulou-Hielscher's "Espace féminin et image divine: vers une définition de la religion dans *Pluie et vent sur Télumée Miracle* de Simone Schwarz-Bart."

15. Claude Karnoouh points out that "the Latin prefix *inter* denotes separation, spacing and reciprocity" (119).

16. In 2016, the European Union includes twenty-eight member states. There are also five candidate countries.

17. "Multiculturalism" refers to the American application of the notion of multiculturality.

18. Welsch is not the first academic to use the term "transcultural." In 1940, Cuban anthropologist Fernando Ortiz used the term "transculturation" for the first time, describing the process of transition from one culture to another. Welsch distinguishes his theory on transculturality from other explanations of the term: "But my usage of the term aims not, as is usual elsewhere, at transcultural constants. With this term I seek rather to take into account the historically altered constitution of today's cultures" ("Transculturality" 31).

19. In a 1991 interview with Lise Gauvin, Edouard Glissant rejects the notion of transculture as one that could supplant his theory of creolization. He explains that the results of transculturation are predictable, whereas creolization and métissage aren't. Glissant highlights the importance of imagination rather than calculation as a way to experience cultural encounters (*L'Imaginaire* 32–33). It is worthwhile to note that Glissant's rejection of transculture predates Welsch's elucidation of transculturality as a cultural theory, so in his interview with Gauvin, Glissant responds to transculture in a general sense rather than Welsch's propos expressed in a later book chapter.

20. "Today's writers, for example, emphasize that their inspirations are shaped not by a single homeland, but by differing reference countries, by French, Austrian, Italian, Russian, South and North American Literature, and so on. Their cultural formation is transcultural" (Welsch, "Transculturality" 24).

2

MOTHERS AND DAUGHTERS

Performing Family Roles in Transcultural Contexts

The previous chapter established the link between Creoleness and trans-culturality, demonstrating the bridges between the two and establishing the usefulness of transculturality in postcolonial literary criticism. That chapter also considered Moudileno's assertion that a "hidden" feminine voice reemerges in Creole literature. This chapter will expand on the manners in which writers express feminine voices through literature, ex-amining the following questions: Does a culturally diverse setting allow for ease of expression of feminine voices? How do mothers interact with family members in such a setting?

Societies with a high concentration of immigration and cultural ex-change tend to invite discussion on the roles of men and women within that society due to the large number of practices and traditions that can exist in a single community. This chapter will examine transculturality as represented by the various mother figures in the works herein. Much as we recognize the existence of an *écriture au féminin*, that is to say, literary works that implicitly or explicitly speak to and about issues perti-nent to women,[1] we can also refer to a transculturality that addresses concerns of women living in a diverse society. These matters include the interaction between men and women in both the private and public spheres, the obstacles faced by an immigrant mother in the host country, and the mother's role in preservation of the native culture in a colonial or postcolonial society. There are undoubtedly intersections and common

interests between masculine and feminine manifestations of transculturality, such as encounters with the hierarchy established by the oppressor
and participation in wars of liberation. Yet, transculturality in a feminine
context is acutely aware of the distinct disadvantages a woman experiences in a postcolonial society, whereas transculturality in a masculine
context will not express those difficulties in depth and with great detail.

As we have already seen, critics such as Condé, Moudileno, and Arnold have pointed out the particularities of Creole literature written by
women, which include depictions of women as guardians of history as
well as the fiber that creates cohesiveness in the family unit. Additionally,
as Moudlieno has noted, these texts do not heed patriarchal discourses,
thus creating literature that turns its attention to events and occurrences
that tell the story of a people, yet are left out by official history (36),
including the cultural significance of food preparation and meals, storytelling, and education of children. It is in this vein that I will explore the
multiple facets of Creoleness, taking into consideration the literary space
inhabited by women writers from the French Caribbean. Simone
Schwarz-Bart and Gisèle Pineau, both Guadeloupian authors, have made
it a point to examine issues that concern the welfare of women in postcolonial societies, where women experience the ravages of natural disasters,
must send their children to work for economic reasons, and endure mari-
tal violence and even incest. This chapter will underline the intersections
between Creoleness and transculturality in the case of women. Likewise,
we will see that it is not only possible but *useful* to identify what could be
called a *"feminine* transculturality," no matter how blurry gender roles
may appear to be.[2] This distinction allows discussion of common experiences portrayed through postcolonial literature and, more specifically and
pertinent to this study, sheds light on some circumstances that foster
creativity on the part of women.

It is true that postcolonial theory often neglects issues related to wom-
en and gender.[3] Considering this fact, it is useful to ask if postcolonial
theory does or could allow for meaningful discussion on the subject of
gender. In her chapter "Francophone women writers and postcolonial
theory," Anne Donadey cites Bhabba as one postcolonial theorist who
either overlooks or ignores gender questions. As highlighted in the previous chapter, Creole theorists too have chosen not to broach the topic of
women and gender, neglecting a domain that could enhance their theories
of creolization. Taking into consideration the mostly unexplored rapport

that exists between Francophone women writers and postcolonial theory, Donadey proposes that one classify the relationship as follows: "Given this situation, it may be more accurate to speak of a certain confluence of interests between Francophone women writers and postcolonial theory, rather than a direct contribution of the former to the latter" (203). It is with this dynamic in mind—one of coexistence and *potential* influence— that we proceed with our examination of mothers in a postcolonial context. While discussion of gender and postcoloniality still lies, at least to a certain extent, in the domain of uncharted territory, this chapter will demonstrate the usefulness of examining the two in conjunction with one another.

Before exploring the complexity of motherhood through transculturality, it is necessary to first consider the concepts of mothers and motherhood as they have been examined in literary theory. In her book *The Mother/Daughter Plot: Narrative, Psychoanalysis, Feminism*, Marianne Hirsch poses several interesting questions that serve as an appropriate starting point for discussing mother figures in literature. First, "What is a mother?" and "What is maternal?" Also, "Is motherhood [an] 'experience' or [an] 'institution?'"[4] Finally, "Is it biological or cultural?" (Hirsch 163). Indeed, not all female voices are maternal, and not all mother figures are positive. Given this, my discussion of maternal figures encompasses any woman who profoundly influences the life of a child.[5] Motherhood is not only biological but also cultural, as each mother figure, in some way, passes history and tradition onto her children.

The performative aspect of motherhood is thus of utmost importance in this examination of Francophone postcolonial mother figures. *Performing Motherhood* by Michèle Longino Farrell examines the correspondence of Madame de Sévigné, discussing the manner in which a mother operates within a patriarchal system. Longino points out that in the seventeenth century, the formation of the mother figure was strongly influenced by male society. The centuries that separate seventeenth-century literature from the contemporary works of Francophone authors have most certainly allowed for evolution of the literary mother figure, but similarities can be seen across the centuries. According to Longino, Madame de Sévigné depicts herself as a mother to assert herself in a society that places little value on mothers of grown children and widows. As we shall see in Ying Chen's *L'Ingratitude*, Gisèle Pineau's *L'espérance-macadam*, and Simone Schwarz-Bart's *Pluie et vent sur Télumée Mira-*

cle, contemporary literary mothers still define themselves in relation to the patriarchy which surrounds them. The act of mothering one's children, whether biological or adopted, continues to be one of the most important ways for a character to define herself in the context of a given society.[6] Like Madame de Sévigné and other subsequent mother figures, such as those portrayed by Colette, Simone de Beauvoir, and Marguerite Duras, postcolonial literary mothers function within societies dominated by men. There are, however, added layers of complexity to those mother figures who also deal with the restraints imposed upon them by their postcolonial societies. They find themselves not only marginalized as women but, linguistically and culturally speaking as well, oftentimes relegated to a purely domestic role with little contact outside the family unit.

Works such as Longino's *Performing Motherhood* and others, including Saint-Martin's "Le nom de la mère: Le rapport mère-fille comme constante de l'écriture au féminin" and *Writing Mothers and Daughters*, edited by Adalgisa Giorgio, provide a solid foundation for studies on mothers in literature, acting as stepping stones for studies on mother figures in a postcolonial context instead of a purely European one. In my examination of mothers from the works of selected authors, I address the following questions: What does the literary depiction of mothers reveal about mothering in a postcolonial, culturally diverse context? How does living in a host country affect the act of mothering? What similarities are there between mother figures of different cultural traditions, heritages, and languages? In short, what parallels can be drawn between the mother figures in different Francophone regions?

MOTHER FIGURES AND THE CONSEQUENCES OF TRANSCULTURALITY

The intricacies of a feminine transculturality as expressed through mother figures can perhaps be best understood in their differentiation from mother figures from the French literary tradition. French literature of the twentieth century abounds with representations of the mother, many of them complex women whose struggles are portrayed through the eyes of their daughter-narrators. Like the mother figures examined in this study, mother figures in French literature are limited by the expectations of a patriarchal society.[7] Yet we shall see that motherhood in a postcolonial context carries burdens not often expressed in French literature.

Colette and Simone de Beauvoir, two writers who influenced feminism and feminist writing in the West, both present loving mothers yet do not hesitate to point out what they perceive to be the disadvantages and risks involved in giving birth and mothering.[8] Colette was a prolific writer and some of her best-loved works focus on the mother. Sido is modeled after Colette's own mother and plays a central role in the collection of short stories *La Maison de Claudine* (1922), the novella *La Naissance du jour* (1928), and the novella *Sido* (1930). She is an attentive, possessive mother who constantly worries about her children. The home and garden comprise her domain, and it is in these places that the mother figure is most fully expressed.

Sido plays a dominant role in the life of the daughter-narrator. In the home and garden, she is queen, and her family does not question the central role she plays within that unit. Although she expresses emotion and is seen in moments of weakness, Sido is undisputedly constructed as a quasi-mythic character. Colette's *Sido* is an homage to the mother in which the author proclaims, "Je la chante, de mon mieux" (22). [I do my best to sing her praises.] This work further develops the persona of Sido through description of interaction with her husband, children, and other people who pass through their lives. Everything can be traced back and even attributed to Sido.

Whereas Colette often puts the mother figure on a pedestal, de Beauvoir uses the mother figure to criticize the middle class woman's traditional role as wife and mother. Many of her works, including *Les Mandarins* (1961), *L'Invitée* (1968), and the play *Les Bouches inutiles* (1945), analyze the mother's role through a rather skeptical, distant lens.[9] She is not in any way idealized, as de Beauvoir's women characters oftentimes illustrate her feminist views annunciated in *Le Deuxième sexe*. Unlike Colette, whose stories document the mother-daughter exchange that defines the monumental relationship between the narrator and her mother, de Beauvoir denies any substantial influence of mothers over their children. A mother's role is *not* to form and educate her children but rather to perform thankless and necessary tasks for them, such as changing diapers (Patterson 345). De Beauvoir's vision of motherhood is therefore considerably narrower than that of Colette, which reflects the differing objectives of the two authors in setting out to write on the mother.

Simone de Beauvoir portrays the mother as a product of a society in which a middle class woman is relegated to child rearing and serving her husband. De Beauvoir's ambivalence about a mother's role is manifest, and the reader can see that the mother is key in the daughter's need for adolescent rebellion and, later, emotional distance. De Beauvoir does not specifically condemn her own mother or mother figures in general, but she does criticize the institution of motherhood and the patriarchal society that creates that institution. De Beauvoir's conception of motherhood is, thus, riddled with trepidation.

One can draw parallels between the mother figures examined in this study and those described by Colette and de Beauvoir. Just as Colette portrays Sido as the dominant figure in the home and garden, Schwarz-Bart and Pineau also paint mothers who reign over the domestic sphere. De Beauvoir's skepticism concerning maternal control is inflated in the accounts of Yan-Zi in *L'Ingratitude* by Ying Chen. These and other commonalities traverse the boundaries of time and place, but the depiction of mothers in highly diverse, contemporary societies serve as a counterpoint to Colette's and de Beauvoir's mother figures. The political and social implications of colonialism and postcolonialism as well as different cultural practices make for a variety of characters who play the mother role in ways more varied than those of the aforementioned authors. Societal changes such as the fall of colonialism paired with increased interaction between those of different cultures have made for an evolution in the mother figure. It is therefore necessary for us to expand our vision of literary mother figures, going beyond the already complex figures of French literature to include the mothers examined in this study.

Representations of mother figures in a transcultural setting reveal that their experiences, some of which include displacement, exile, and wars of liberation, are not always affirming. On the contrary, motherhood in a transcultural society depicts traumas not often expressed in French literature. Although they do not focus specifically on mother figures, Simon Harel's studies on Quebecois society and literature underscore the potentially traumatic downfalls of life in exile: "La mémoire de l'émigrant et de ses descendants est soumise à l'événement d'un choc traumatique et à sa profonde et sévère résonance. De ce choc résulte un interdit d'habiter qui plonge le sujet dans le plus vif désarroi" (176). [The memory of the emigrant and his descendants is subject to the occurrence of a traumatic shock and to its profound and severe resonance. This shock results in an inability to live that plunges the subject into the most vivid disarray.] The effects of the traumatic shock referenced by Harel, weaved into the works treated in this study, end up sparking creative acts that demonstrate a specifically "feminine" transculturality.

For instance, the passing on of traditions from mother to child is a predominant theme in both French and Francophone writing. Yet in a colonial or postcolonial society, the oppressor has the power to undermine the native culture, thus creating a hierarchy of cultures. In *La Femme sans sépulture*, Assia Djebar portrays Zoulikha, mother of four and combatant in Algeria's war of liberation. Educated in French colonial schools, she rejects both the French and traditional Algerian patriarchies in refusing to wear the veil and joining the war effort against the French. She experiences firsthand the hierarchal structure of the colonies, and in rejecting that system, she sets an example for her children who, later in life, will live in Algeria's postcolonial society. Francophone mother figures like Zoulikha must negotiate multiple cultures and languages, striving to find a balance between acceptance in a society dominated by the oppressor and survival of their own ways. The overwhelming presence of another culture is a fact of life that risks stamping out their own cultural practices and religious beliefs. Through interaction with her children, however, the mother plays a small part in saving her culture from extinction. Her role as guardian of culture is thus an urgent one, [10] with pressures that Western mother figures may not experience.

Family dynamics are also altered by the effects of transculturality, as illustrated by the high number of women who serve as heads of household. Unlike Colette and de Beauvoir, most Francophone authors do not portray traditional nuclear families, reflecting the phenomenon of single parenthood that so often reins in some postcolonial societies. Maryse Condé has remarked that men are currently taking on more active roles in families in the Caribbean (Thomas 170), yet one cannot deny that at least in postcolonial literature, they are often overshadowed by their female counterparts. In Gisèle Pineau's *L'espérance-macadam*, Eliette adopts a young girl who has been molested by her father, accepting the responsibility of raising Angela on her own. *L'Ingratitude*, by Ying Chen, portrays an incompetent, voiceless father who always bends to the will of his wife, and in *La Femme sans sépulture*, by Assia Djebar, the vibrant Zoulikah outshines her successive husbands. The relative unimportance and virtual invisibility of strong male figures seems to render their presence unnecessary in the context of a postcolonial family. Contemporary Francophone texts therefore criticize the patriarchy in ways not pertinent to the works of previous French authors through creation of households that manage to function and sometimes thrive in spite of their "manless" state.[11] While the mother figures of Colette and de Beauvoir garner plenty of attention and sometimes admiration from their daughter-narrators, father figures do play a necessary, productive role in the family unit, both financially and morally. This is most definitely not the case in the works at hand, where fragmented families are the norm and where absence is a dominant characteristic of family life. Mother figures both directly and indirectly present a challenge to the patriarchal systems that have inhibited them emotionally, sexually, and professionally. Whereas Colette's and de Beauvoir's discourses concern sexual liberation and economic independence in a *Western* society, those of Francophone writers involve battles against certain aspects of that very western society—one whose imposed and unjust political system stifles and exploits a whole population linguistically, religiously, physically, politically, and economically.

Keeping in mind the inherent differences mentioned above, it is possible and worthwhile to discuss both French mother figures as well as those in transcultural settings as victims of a patriarchal society. There are, however, distinct sets of circumstances, brought on by colonialism and postcolonialism, from which new sorts of literary mother figures emerge and which invite discussion of transculturality as it is experienced by women.

DISPLACEMENT AND TRANSCULTURAL ENCOUNTERS

Postcolonial literature stems, in part, from a history of invasion and displacement. Literature of the French Caribbean, for example, is keenly aware of the slave trade that brought Africans to the Caribbean as well as the European invasion of the islands, practically wiping out the native population. These historical facts have played and continue to play an important role in Creole society and consequently in the literature of the region. My study focuses heavily on the characteristics of transcultural societies and how they influence representation of mother figures in literature. Consideration of the French Caribbean, however, lends itself to discussions of both interculturality and transculturality, as examination of various texts will illustrate.[12]

Schwarz-Bart and Pineau's mother figures, although different from one another, are all products of the islands' history. While they could be considered victims of the unpleasant circumstances of their lives, each is a strong and imposing figure for her children. As is often the case in Creole literature, the principal mother figure is the grandmother or an adopted mother figure, as we see in Pineau's *L'espé rance-macadam*. Whether the mother resides in her native village or in a large city far from home, Schwarz-Bart's and Pineau's mother figures each display numerous characteristics that demonstrate an awareness of other cultures. In the case of Schwarz-Bart, mother figures perceive otherness yet have limited interaction with those of varied backgrounds. Rather, they simply possess the knowledge that their ancestors are from elsewhere and that there are stark differences between them and the French, who are at the top of the Antillean social ladder. This awareness endows Schwarz-Bart's novels with an intercultural perspective, since little mixing and exchange occur between people of different social, economic, and ethnic backgrounds.

In Schwarz-Bart's novel *Pluie et Vent*, Reine Sans Nom showers her granddaughter with love and support as she grows up, falls in love, and then is abused and left by her husband. Well into Télumée's adulthood, she is a constant, steady presence. She gives Télumée wise counsel as her granddaughter navigates young married life: "Nous, les Lougandor, ne craignons pas davantage le bonheur que le malheur, ce qui signifie que tu as le devoir aujourd'hui de te réjouir sans appréhension ni retenue" (PV 142). [We, the Lougandors, don't fear happiness any more than unhappiness, which means that today it is your duty to rejoice without apprehension, without restraint.] In spite of the racism and poverty that she experiences, Reine Sans Nom consistently conveys a message of empowerment to her granddaughter. Her wisdom and insight into human nature don't come from extensive interaction with outsiders, yet she and other residents of the village are curious about the *Békés*, descendants of the French colonizers and the wealthiest people on the island. When Télumée works for the affluent Desaragne family, she is peppered with questions during her occasional visits home:

> Les gens voulaient savoir comment se déroulait la vie à Belle-Feuille, derrière tous ces remparts de verdure, à quoi ressemblait l'intérieur de

l'habitation, comment on y mangeait, parlait, buvait, menait le train-train de la vie quotidienne et surtout: qu'est-ce qui compte pour eux dans l'existence, et sont-ils au moins contents de vivre ? . . . (PV 103–104).

[People wanted to know how life was at Belle-Feuille, behind all the walls of greenery, what the inside of the house looked like, how they ate, talked, drank, dealt with daily routine and above all: what counts for them in life, and are they at least content to live? . . .]

The residents of Fond-Zombi have limited experience with and knowledge of the Békés, and so the mystery surrounding white people sparks conversation and contemplation. *Pluie et vent* displays little enmeshment between the French and the descendants of slaves, yet they do intermingle, co-exist, and wonder about the other.

Whereas Reine Sans Nom uplifts her granddaughter, the mother figure in *Un plat de porc* reinforces feelings of shame that haunt Mariotte. Although much of this study focuses on that of mothering in a culturally diverse context, *Un Plat de porc* also brings to light complexities of "daughtering" in such circumstances. As discussed in the first chapter of this study, Mariotte spends the last years of her life in a Paris nursing home, far from her roots in the Caribbean. Although she aches to return to Martinique, her imagination only provides her with painful encounters with long gone family members. When Mariotte begins interacting with figures from her past, the specter of her grandmother chides her now-elderly granddaughter for addressing her in French rather than Creole. Ashamed, Mariotte remarks, "Toute vidée de tristesse, réduite à néant, je ne sais que répéter de mon ancienne voix de petite fille: *Aïe mémé chè, aïe toute-douce an moin.* . . . Qui prétend que je ne sais plus parler le créole? . . . Quel diable a bien pu vous mettre en tête cette fausseté?" (PP 48). [All empty from sadness, reduced to nothing, all I can do is repeat in my former little girl's voice: *Aïe mémé chè, aïe toute-douce an moin.* . . . Who says that I no longer know how to speak Creole? . . . What devil could have given you this falsity?"][13] Mariotte's defensive response to her grandmother's reproach demonstrates her acute shame regarding her disconnection from her culture of origin. She seeks and speaks the Creole terms of endearment that remain from her childhood, and she is quick to point out to her grandmother's spirit that she has not forgotten her native language. Her need to access her past is a strong one, but she does so tentatively in her daydreams, aware of the years and distance that separate her from her family.

Mariotte, nearing the end of her own life, perceives Mémé Louise as an intolerant, mean-spirited mother figure who does not understand her granddaughter. Her grandmother reminds Mariotte of her place in society: "Par la maudicité du sang! . . . Combien de fois ne t'ai-je pas mise en garde: reste à ta place de négresse, ma fille, n'en bouge pas d'une corde; sinon le monde blanc va t'écraser comme un simple margouillat?" (PP 48). [Bloody hell! . . . How many times have I warned you: stay in your place of a black woman, my daughter, don't move an inch; otherwise the white world will smash you like a simple lizard?] A former slave, Mémé Louise's understanding of the black woman's role is one of passivity and caution. She perceives whites as capable of squashing her granddaughter like a pest. Yet, the specter of the grandmother is also mean. In fleeing the tension of the nursing home through intentional hallucination, Mariotte succumbs to worries and complexes that manifest themselves in the image of a vindictive grandmother who spits on her granddaughter, reminding Mariotte that she was "mal sortie . . . venue au monde avec des cheveux trop crépus, une peau trop violacée, d'épaisses narines qui déparaient" (PP 52). [a sorry sight . . . came to the earth with hair that was too kinky, skin too blue, thick nostrils that marred {the face}.] Mariotte's imaginary encounters with her grandmother are upsetting on multiple levels. Mémé Louise reminds her of the shameful heritage of slavery. She admires and emulates the ways of her western master, neglecting and condemning her own history and the value system of her people. This is troubling for Mariotte, not only because she is aware of the suffering of her ancestors but also because she has not fully overcome the shameful legacy of domination. Like the spirit of her grandmother, Mariotte has inherited and bought into the discourse of her oppressors. During her lucid moments, she harshly criticizes many aspects of French culture, such as the cruel treatment that she and the other residents receive at the hands of their caretakers, as well as the fact that white people place the elderly in nursing homes in the first place (PP 12, 153). Mariotte is nevertheless unable to shed her shameful associations of inferiority, as evidenced by her frequent imagined and bitter returns to her childhood. Rather, she remarks that she is eternally lost in the dark and cold world of white people (PP 39).

In Mariotte's old age, her long-term displacement colors the way in which she acts out her daughter role. She is desperate to rekindle lost family connections, but the interactions she conjures remind her of the shame of her past. Furthermore, while her distance from her family may not have exacerbated her feelings of inferiority, she has, at the very least, maintained problematic and unequal relationships with Europeans. In spite of her decades-long absence from her native island, she has been unable to fully break away from the behaviors she learned as a child. Even as an elderly woman, she bends to the will of her white peers.

Why does Mariotte waver in the face of her oppressor while Reine Sans Nom and Télumée maintain their calm and inner strength? To what can we contribute the contrasting reactions to difference as experienced by these mothers and daughters? The answer to these questions may lie in the exile experience. Reine Sans Nom and Télumée spend their whole lives in Guadeloupe. In spite of the hardships they face, including violence, abandonment, and poverty, they remain firmly attached to their island and to the identities they form there. Mariotte, on the other hand, has experienced the trauma of displacement and migration, reminding us of Harel's assertion that life in exile incites a debilitating shock.[14] Each day in the shared space of the retirement home, Mariotte encounters Europeans who reveal the stereotypes they hold about people of African origins, such as Monsieur Moreau who calls her "ma Doudou" (PP 36). It is true that in this transcultural setting, Mariotte experiences more diversity in her everyday encounters than she would have had she never left Martinique. Yet, in living out this transcultural existence, she has surrendered the stable identity that life on her island may have afforded her.

STORMY SOCIETY, FERTILE FUTURE

Much like *Un plat de porc*, Pineau's novel *L'espérance-macadam* demonstrates the complexities of transculturality. Eliette is characterized by, to borrow the words of Moisan, "à la fois le passage et le changement d'un lieu, d'un état ou d'un moment, à un autre" (208). [at the same time passage and change of place, from one state or one moment, to another.] This mother figure is eternally linked to the physical and emotional passages she has undergone to arrive at the present moment. Upheaval has defined her as a human being and has heavily influenced the way in which she enacts her maternal role. Married and widowed three times, Eliette is a resident of Guadeloupe's Savane Mulet,[15] a place of refuge for many undesirables:

> Au fur et à mesure, dans les années soixante, la plupart des esprits mauvais furent refoulés sur l'autre bord de la rivière. Et une multitude peupla soudain Savane. Ils arrivaient de partout, barraient des morceaux de terre, plantaient des cases immondes. . . . Gens jetés de tous les côtés de Guadeloupe. (EM 24)

> [Little by little, in the 60s, most of the bad eggs were pushed to the other side of the river. And suddenly multitudes populated Savane. They arrived from everywhere, blocked off pieces of land, planted squalid huts. . . . People thrown from all parts of Guadeloupe.]

Savane Mulet protects Eliette from the violent memories of a cyclone in which she was injured and which she believes to have left her infertile. It is a place which lets her forget and, when she is ready, remember traumatic events of her life. Although unable to conceive a child, she eventually adopts a neighbor girl who has been sexually abused by her father. Thus, Savane Mulet is also a space that allows her to become a mother. Like Mémé Louise and Reine Sans Nom, Eliette experiences interculturality, or the co-existence of cultures, in her people's history of displacement and slavery. Her transcultural experience is represented in the fact that she herself has sought refuge in Savane Mulet after having lived through an event that very well could have taken her life. The community offers a high degree of cultural diversity and welcomes people from different regions and walks of life. In Savane Mulet, dubbed *Quartier-Mélo* by a French police officer,[16] Eliette encounters people with roots in both English- and Spanish-speaking areas (EM 24–25). The community of Savane Mulet never attains a harmonious existence, and Eliette is witness to the agony that permeates the area: "Les paroles se sont mises à voltiger dans mon salon. Querelles, cris, pleurs, rires, tambours me tenaient éveillée dans la couche jusque tard dans la nuit. Ma case, au coeur de Savane Mulet, était devenue comme un grand bénitier plein des vies démontées des nations assemblées" (EM 26). [Words took to flying about in my living room. Quarrels, cries, tears, laughter, drums kept me awake in bed until late in the night. My hut, in the heart of Savane Mulet, had become like a big baptismal font full of the dismantled lives of the assembled nations]. Although Eliette does not actively seek contact with the other residents of *Quartier-Mélo*, she does serve to witness and chronicle the traumatisms that define life in the settlement. Her transcultural experience is formed not only through person-to-person interaction outside the home, but perhaps more importantly through contemplation of the diverse and troubled society she observes from the safety of her living room. Yet poverty and crime create an environment of distrust and suspicion, so the transculturality that Eliette and the other residents know is a troubled one that does not adhere to Welsch's vision of transcultural societies.

The negative aspects of life in Savane Mulet, including poverty, filth, and violence, make for an unpleasant existence that exudes dishonesty. People from all over the Caribbean have settled in the area, have come to know their neighbors, and yet have never come to fully trust one another. This proves to be one of the drawbacks of displacement and consequently of transculturality—the inability to trust others with different backgrounds and personal histories. Eliette cannot help but be influenced by her community, yet she seeks solitude: "Eliette cherchait rien d'autre sur cette terre que la paix de sa case. Pas mêler son existence au désordre de Savane. Pas laisser son esprit donner couleurs aux sons, bâtir des cathédrales de douleur en son cœur" (EM 8). [Eliette sought nothing other on this earth than the peace of her hut. Not mixing her existence with the disorder of Savane. Not allowing her mind to give colors to the sounds, building cathedrals of pain in her heart.] Although Eliette has attempted to isolate herself from the crimes, abuse, and heartbreak that have repeatedly occurred in her community, the sordid atmosphere of Savane Mulet has inhibited her for years. Yet when she finally opens her eyes to Angela's grave situation, one which parallels her own adolescent memories, she knows she must reach out to the girl. For Eliette, a transcultural society proves to be a double-edged sword. On the one hand, discomfort and mistrust of others cause her to retreat into her private space, but on the other hand, that very same society presents her with the opportunity for and responsibility of motherhood, a role she has actively sought throughout her adult life.

Much like Mariotte, Eliette's story demonstrates the fact that displacement is not only an historical fact of postcolonial literature but also a contemporary reality. Living in exile is a prevalent theme in Francophone literature, and what Welsch refers to as "new forms of entanglement" ("Transculturality" 23) resulting from migration contribute to the transcultural nature of much of today's literature. The word *entanglement* is especially pertinent in consideration of Mariotte's and Eliette's stories, as both of them are ensnared in situations where otherness influences the way they see themselves and understand the world around them.

The novels treated in this study attest to the fact that women, and especially mothers living in exile, find themselves in an unenviable position as they raise their families in postcolonial contexts. Djebar writes about immigrant women as balancing between two silences (*Ces voix* 202), and Farid Laroussi notes that Algerian feminine discourse formed during the war of liberation has been forgotten or hidden (189). Yet, time and again, women's eclipsed voices emerge through literature. In spite of their trials, the entanglements of transcultural societies *can* prove to be a stimulating and creative force.

EXILE AND INNER SPACE

Abla Farhoud's first novel, *Le bonheur a la queue glissante*, exhibits the effects of demographic upheaval on women as well as a resulting act of literary creation. *Le bonheur a la queue glissante*, exemplifies many characteristics of transculturality, as it deals with exile, language barriers, preservation of culture, and acceptance in and of the host culture. There are several levels of transculturality expressed in this novel, as demonstrated in the relationships Dounia maintains with her children and her husband. Her interactions with her husband are peppered with memories of physical violence and emotional neglect, and her first years in Canada marked by isolation: "Je ne pouvais parler à personne. Je ne connaissais pas la langue du pays, je ne sortais jamais de la maison, je n'avais ni parents ni amies, mon mari avait tellement de problèmes, c'était impossible de lui parler" (BQ 31). [I couldn't talk to anyone. I didn't know the country's language, I never left the house, I didn't have family or friends, my husband had so many problems, it was impossible to talk to him.] Abuse, loneliness, and the inability to communicate underscore the struggles of Dounia's life in a transcultural society. The relationships she maintains with her children, however, demonstrate the success they have achieved in life as both parents and young professionals, at ease in various cultural and social situations. While Dounia was not able to overcome the barriers to integration, her children were. She therefore experiences and embodies both positive and negative aspects of transculturality.

Since leaving Lebanon with her small children to join her husband in Canada, Dounia has experienced numerous obstacles in raising her family abroad and has come to the realization that for her, "home" is with family rather than with place, land, country, or a given nation-state: "Certains immigrants disent: 'Je voudrais mourir là où je suis né.' Moi, non. Mon pays, ce n'est pas le pays de mes ancêtres ni même le village de mon enfance, mon pays, c'est là où mes enfants sont heureux" (BQ 22). [Certain immigrants say: "I would like to die where I was born." As for me, no. My country, it's neither the country of my ancestors nor the village of my childhood, my country, it's where my children are happy.] Although she never escapes the feeling of living in exile, Dounia knows from experience that she cannot return to her homeland without feeling like an outsider. In Canada, she has difficulty communicating with those outside her immediate family, as she speaks neither French nor English. In Lebanon, where one would expect her to feel at ease, she has lost her personal connections. Upon her family's return, they are considered "American" and are therefore outsiders (BQ 109). Dounia's identity, like those of other immigrants, cannot be defined within the framework of a nation. She has experienced multiple displacements, all forced, and so the way in which she situates herself in a particular space is more important than her country of origin or even her country of residence. Simon Harel defines this phenomenon as *la pensée-habitacle* (123). Dounia's *lieu habité*, that is to say, the space she inhabits, more readily and accurately captures her identity and better allows for self-expression than would description of a claimed homeland.[17]

Having immigrated proves to have been the seminal event of Dounia's life: "La chose qui a été la plus importante de toute ma vie? C'est . . . attends . . . laisse-moi réfléchir . . . Je dirais que c'est d'avoir émigré. Oui. Avoir changé de pays. Parce que cela a complètement changé ma vie et celle de mes enfants" (BQ 121). [The thing that's been the most important in all of my life? It's . . . wait . . . let me think . . . I would say that it's having emigrated. Yes. Having changed countries. Because that completely changed my life and that of my children's.] The life she has lived in Canada can hardly be compared to the one she would have led in Lebanon.

Dounia has, however, been able to incorporate bits of her culture into her life in exile. One element she has passed on is her Arab proverbs, sprinkled in conversation at appropriate moments: "Un proverbe vient en temps et lieu, en accord ou en désaccord avec ce qui vient d'être dit ou fait" (BQ 23). [A proverb comes at the right time and place, in agreement or disagreement with what has just been said or done]. Nathalie Buchet Rogers posits that the inclusion of proverbs in texts from traditionally oral cultures represents the tension between the oral culture and a written culture that threatens to infiltrate and transform it (435). I would add that in *Le Bonheur a la queue glissante*, the proverbs that Dounia utters are also a reminder of the tension that exists between the silence in which she has existed for decades and the hectic, chatty universe of her offspring. At the end of the novel when she is living in a retirement home, Dounia admits that "Le silence est lourd à porter, comme un corps sans vie" (BQ 158). [The silence is heavy to bear, like a lifeless body]. As much as silence proves to burden her, it also serves as a protective barrier that allows her to avoid painful topics. At another point, Dounia admits that her use of proverbs allows her to evade potentially uncomfortable situations: "Je réponds par un dicton, un proverbe ou une phrase toute faite quand mes enfants me posent une question sur mon passé, c'est plus facile que d'avoir à chercher la vérité, à la dire, à la revivre" (BQ 30). [I respond with a dictum, a proverb, or a canned expression when my children ask me a question about my past, it's easier than having to search for the truth, to speak it, to relive it.] Swiss philosopher Max Picard notes: "In silence the truth is passive and slumbering, but in language it is wide awake" (31). For Dounia, the sharing of proverbs serves as a brief escape from the inner place where truth sleeps, but their brevity allows her to quickly retreat back into that place of silence.

Her frequent use of proverbs demonstrates a way in which she chooses to operate in her *pensée-habitacle*. The nuggets of truth provide her with a means of instruction without having to delve into unhappy moments from her past: *Ce que l'oeil n'a pas vu, l'intelligence peut l'imaginer.* [That which the eye did not see, intelligence can imagine.]; *Rends les choses difficiles, elles le seront; facilite-les, elles deviendront faciles.* [Make things difficult, they'll be difficult; ease them, they'll become easy.]; *Le bonheur a la queue glissante.* [Happiness has a slippery tail].[18] As a means of expression, the poetic nature of proverbs fosters contemplation and discourages immediate response or questioning.

Myriam, one of Dounia's daughters, has become attached to the proverbs that have served as a sort of auditory background in her relationship with her mother.[19] She collects the proverbs in a notebook and aspires to tell her mother's story, which we can assume is Farhoud's novel, told in the mother's voice. Myriam's affinity for the proverbs proves not only the potency of her mother's words but also reflects her desire to understand Dounia.

In *Le bonheur a la queue glissante*, Farhoud gives voice to a mother sheathed in a silence that is both lonely and protective. Like many of the mother figures examined in this study, Dounia spends much of her life in a culture not her own. We have seen that for women and specifically mothers, living in a culturally rich environment can lead to isolation and introspection. If *presence* in a new culture influences expression, how might *absence* from one's culture of origin and family affect self-examination? In that vein, how might absence encourage a woman to emerge from her silence?

TRANSCULTURALITY AND ABSENCE

As mentioned early in this chapter, loss, death, and trauma are common concerns in postcolonial literature. In the context of geographical displacement or death, family members are left behind, mourning the loss of a loved one. Questions concerning personal history go unanswered, and separation from one's family and past brings on sadness and confusion. Absent father figures are common in literature. But as seen in the novels of Simone Schwarz-Bart, there is also room for discussion of mothers and children whose absence upsets the family unit. *La Femme sans sépulture* by Assia Djebar, *Des rêves et des assassins* by Malika Mokeddem, and *L'Ingratitude* by Ying Chen each present women who are, for one reason or another, absent from family life. In each of these novels, one family member's physical absence creates concrete and specific situations that leave family members to search, wonder, and spin tales about what may have happened to their loved ones.

Zoulikha, *la femme sans sépulture*,[20] left her young children with their older sister to fight in Algeria's war of liberation. The narrator of the story returns to Zoulikha's city Césarée, also the narrator's home town, to make a documentary about the heroine. Years after Zoulikha's disappearance and Algeria's independence, her daughters still suffer in their mother's absence and perceived abandonment.[21] Hania, the eldest, explains to the narrator, "Si je parle d'elle, je me soulage, je me débarasse des dents de l'amertume. Oh, je sais bien, les autres femmes de la ville, aujourd'hui, pensent que je suis fière de Zoulikha" (FS 51). [In speaking of her, I comfort myself, I get rid of the sharp bitterness. Oh, I know, the other women in the city, today, think that I am proud of Zoulikha.] She does not deny the deep connection between herself and her mother, but it seems that she has yet to accept her mother's abandonment, death, and the fact that she did not receive a proper burial.[22] "Plusieurs fois je vis, dans un rêve, sa sépulture: illuminé, isolé, un monument superbe, et je pleurais sans fin devant ce mausolée" (FS 61). [Numerous times I saw, in a dream, her sepulcher: illuminated, isolated, a superb monument, and I was crying endlessly in front of the mausoleum.] Hania has no tomb to visit and therefore feels that she has no way to pay tribute to or confide in her deceased mother. She believes that she and her sister are "plus défavorisées que de simples orphelines" (FS 93). [more unlucky than regular orphans.] In Hania's life, grief intertwines with resentment. Zoulikha's absence and disappearance have robbed her daughter of the mother-daughter dialogue she desires.

Although less vocal than her older sister, Mina also has difficulty dealing with her mother's absence and status as war hero. During her summer vacation she returns to her sister's house from Algiers, and in the afternoons she visits Dame Lionne, a friend of her mother's. In the hours the two women spend together, the talkative Dame Lionne delves into the past, rehashing stories about her friendship with Zoulikha. For Dame Lionne and the other women who knew Zoulikha, the act of storytelling becomes a way to reconstruct the many facets of this heroine's persona, but in a broader sense, a way to piece together a history of women's involvement in the war of liberation. It is difficult for Mina to hear Dame Lionne's stories about her mother: "Qu'elle ne me parle pas aujourd'hui . . . de ma mère! Je ne veux plus trembler, ni souffrir!" (FS 27). [I hope that she doesn't speak to me today . . . of my mother! I don't want to tremble, to suffer anymore.] In spite of her reticence to listen to stories about Zoulikha, Mina seeks the company of Dame Lionne. While Hania voices a residual bitterness concerning their mother, the younger sister admits that it is painful to hear people speak of the heroine. The sisters react differently to their mother's absence. The elder daughter, who knew and remembers their mother best, yearns for her presence. To the contrary, the younger daughter expresses a preference for silence regarding Zoulikha. Yet the protective silence that she desires isn't possible, as Mina surrounds herself with women who continue to honor her deceased mother through the sharing of memories.

Like her daughters, the spectral mother grapples with the silence that accompanies death. An interesting characteristic of the novel is the presence of Zoulikha's four monologues, addressed to Mina, where her spirit attempts to explain her decision to leave her family, shed light on the circumstances of her death, and provide guidance for her youngest daughter.[23] Her four monologues, contributed by a spectral narrator and interspersed throughout the text, represent an attempt at mothering beyond the grave, as the spirit shares stories that she would have shared with Mina, had she been alive. In the third monologue, for example, she tells about meeting Mina's father, the ten happy years they spent together, and then how their lives changed once he was killed (FS 190–193). The monologues also reveal information about Zoulikha's last days and the mother-son relationships she developed with some of the young men with whom she served (FS 230). In his article "Place, Position, and Postcolonial Haunting in Assia Djebar's *La Femme sans sépulture*," Michael O'Riley notes that Djebar's use of spectral voice reappropriates history while avoiding the problem of the "imperialist gesture of appropriation and effacement so related to place" (66). On a similar note, Zoulikha's ghostly monologues seek to reappropriate the maternal duties she sacrificed in death. The deceased mother figure finds a voice and tries to perform the act of motherhood for her youngest daughter. Sadly, Mina doesn't acknowledge her mother, and in the last paragraph of the novel Zoulikha tells her daughter where she can be found: "Une clairière, ma chérie, où tu ne viendras jamais. N'importe, c'est sur la place du douar, la voix de l'inconnue chantant inlassablement, c'est là, yeux ouverts, dans tout mon corps pourrissant, que je t'attends" (FS 234). [A clearing, sweetheart, where you'll never come. No matter, it's on the douar square, the voice of the unknown woman singing tirelessly, it's there, eyes open, in my rotting body, that I await you.] As her spirit seeks to erase the boundaries between life and death in an effort to mother her daughter, Zoulikha also fulfills a more encompassing role, that of inscribing history.

We know that transculturality deals with the disappearance of boundaries and intermingling of cultures that form many contemporary literary characters, yet this does not exclude conflict and violence. During her life, Zoulikha encountered multiple cultures that are important to address in consideration of this mother figure. Educated in French colonial schools, Zoulikha chose to leave her family and fight for Algerian independence. The interplay between cultures is fundamental in the formation of this unique character. We learn that her desire to be free and adventurous is in conflict with Algerian society's wish that she veil herself or remain in the home. The fact that she had three husbands also goes against society's expectations for a woman. In keeping with her contradictory ways, she chose to put her life on the line and fight the colonial power. Zoulikha is a very different kind of mother who refuses to accept traditional roles yet respects and maintains friendships with those who do. Her legendary and spectral status differentiate her from other mother figures examined in this study.

MOTHERLESS WANDERING

Mokeddem's *Des rêves et des assassins* also presents a motherless Algerian girl. Kenza is raised in her diabolic father's household and has no memory of her mother, whom she has not seen since the age of two and who has since passed away. She is aware of certain facts pertaining to Keltoum, her mother. Kenza was born in Montpellier, France, the year of Algeria's independence, when her mother was in the country caring for an ailing brother. Upon her return to Algeria, Keltoum discovered that her husband had taken a second wife and that the couple was expecting a child. She left, and her husband prevented her from taking Kenza with her: "J'avais trois mois lorsque, sur le seuil d'une porte, mon père m'arracha à ses bras" (RA 10). [I was three months old then, on the threshold of a door, my father tore me from her arms.] Most of what Kenza knows about her mother is vague, such as details concerning her apparent "kidnapping":

> Il paraît que ma mère m'a enlevée lors de l'un de ses retours à Oran. Que pendant quinze jours mon père a écumé la ville et battu son épouse. Il paraît qu'on m'a retrouvé en bas de l'immeuble, le jour où ma mère reprit le bateau pour la France. J'avais deux ans. Il paraît que, par la suite, toutes ses tentatives pour me revoir restèrent vaines. (RA 17)

[It appears that my mother kidnapped me during one of her returns to
Oran. That for two weeks my father searched high and low and beat
his wife. It appears that someone found me downstairs in the building,
the day that my mother took the boat for France. I was two years old. It
appears that, after that, all of her attempts to see me were in vain.]

Kenza's repeated use of *il para ît* insists on the fact that she has doubts
about the official version of the story as it was told to her and that the
truth about her mother is out of reach, given the scant details provided to
her.

One last bit of information about her mother arrives one day, when
Kenza is told by a neighbor child that there is a woman waiting for her in
the street who wants to talk to her about her mother. Zana Baki, a friend
of her mother's, comes bearing the news of her mother's death. Keltoum's tomb is in Oran, and Zana proposes to take Kenza to visit it. At
the burial site, the young girl feels no emotion: "Je n'avais jamais vu
frémir ces traits. N'avais aucun souvenir de baiser, aucune parcelle de vie
commune à insuffler à ce mot: mère. Il ne m'était que l'absence et
l'inconnu. L'absence d'une inconnue. . . . Je ne pouvais pas perdre une
mère que je n'avais jamais eue" (RA 18). [I had never seen her features
quiver. Had no memory of a kiss, no fragment of a shared life to breathe
life into this word: mother. It was only absence and unknown. The absence of a stranger. . . . I couldn't lose a mother I'd never had.] The
child's reaction or lack thereof is directly linked to the fact that she has
absolutely no memory of her mother. Unlike Hania in *La Femme sans
sépulture*, Kenza's access to her mother's burial site is of no importance
to the young girl, since she has no knowledge of the person that her
mother was or what it even means to have a mother. Contrary to Zoulikha's status as legendary figure in Algeria's war of independence, Keltoum is known to few, and her status in her former husband's household
is one of hushed tones and shame. This, of course, filters down to Kenza,
and throughout her childhood she is always set apart from her half brothers and sisters and sent away to boarding school as early as possible.

Both Kenza and her deceased mother are familiar with life in culturally diverse settings. Born on the other side of the Mediterranean, Kenza
has an instant connection to both France and Algeria. When, as a young
woman, she travels to Montpellier in search of information about her
mother, she recognizes the ambivalence of her transcultural experience:

"Gare de Montpellier. Ville étrangère où je suis née. Où ma mère est morte. Un lieu, un lien entre ma naissance et sa mort. Point de rupture de nos deux vies, aussi" (RA 81). [Montpellier train station. Foreign city where I was born. Where my mother died. A place, a connection between my birth and her death. Point of rupture between our two lives, also.] She is thirsty for knowledge about her absent mother and seeks to know her through people who may have crossed her path and landmarks that she would have seen when going about her daily life. At the age of eight, when she learns of her mother's death, she does not feel the need to know about this absent mother figure. Later in life, however, her need to understand her mother propels her across the Mediterranean to a city and country she does not know but to which she is nonetheless linked. In her article "Traversée de l'angoisse et poétique de l'espoir chez Malika Mokeddem," Margot Miller analyzes mobility as a means of fostering and maintaining hope in the search for one's identity (116). Although Miller's article does not refer to *Des rêves et des assassins*, her scholarship most definitely pertains to the path Kenza forges for herself. This protagonist's need to know and understand her deceased mother can only be satisfied through a voyage to another continent, visiting a town that is foreign yet somehow familiar. Kenza's stay in Montpellier sparks ambivalent emotions—the satisfaction of knowing that her mother loved and cared for her paired with the trauma of knowing that she lived a solitary life and died alone after an illegal abortion.

Once she has learned all she can about her mother's painful life and has begun to come to terms with the perceived maternal abandonment, Kenza discovers a need to continue moving, visiting other places in her personal quest: "Il me prend des envies de voyage. Des envies d'aller vers des pays où je n'ai aucune racine" (RA 155). [I feel the need to travel. Need to go towards countries where I have no roots.] As the title of Miller's article indicates, agony and hope go hand in hand in this transformative period. The discoveries Kenza makes in Montpellier are simultaneously cathartic and traumatic, reinforcing the dual nature of her transcultural experience. Kenza's desire to travel hints at a need to mold herself in a neutral space, one Orlando dubs "l'espace d'une métissée" ("Ecriture d'un autre lieu" 105). [the space of a métisse.] Travel and discovery of new places thus become essential to Kenza's identity formation.

The legacies of Zoulikha and Keltoum, both absent, both deceased, both Algerian mothers, affect their children differently. Hania and Mina feel the presence of their mother in Césarée, where she is revered as a hero. Both women also have concrete memories of their mother (FS 51–65, FS 99–111). Kenza's mother, on the other hand, has been almost totally absent from her life, to the extent that Kenza is not even permitted to speak of her (RA 19). The truth about her mother's life in Montpellier and her death at a young age are cloaked in mystery. Kenza benefits from absolutely no mothering beyond the grave and can remember no lessons learned from her mother. While Hania and Mina can tap into memories of their mother and talk about her with people who knew Zoulikha, Kenza's only possibility of rediscovering her mother is to cross the Mediterranean and seek out clues that could help her unravel the secrecy that surrounds Keltoum.

SUICIDE AND YEARNING

Death and absence are also central themes to Ying Chen's novel *L'Ingratitude*, but in this story a daughter disappears from her suffocating mother's life by committing suicide, as she sees it as the only way to escape her mother's influence. The narrator, Yan-Zi, starts her story looking down on her corpse in the morgue, commenting on the way her body is treated and revealing the fact that she committed suicide: "Ma mort est une honte démesurée, car je m'y suis condamnée moi-même, j'en ai exécuté la peine moi-même" (IG 9). [My death is a disproportionate shame, because I condemned myself, I executed the punishment myself.] The tale she weaves is compelling not only because she tells about her suicide and the events leading up to that moment but also because *L'Ingratitude* treats the afterlife as a reality. The existence of life after death is significant for the narrator in that her memories follow her beyond the grave. She never attains a complete separation from the detested mother figure, carrying her earthly traumas into the afterlife, an unsettling situation she had not expected. As Emile J. Talbot remarks in his article "Conscience et mémoire: Ying Chen et la problématique identitaire," for Yan-Zi, "la liberté, même dans la mort, n'est qu'illusion" (152). [liberty, even in death, is only an illusion.] Rather than free her from the burdens that hinder her development as a young woman, Yan-Zi's suicide lances her into a strange space in which she has to deal with those same issues. In *Histoire de fantômes*, Martine Delvaux studies the spectral nature of characters, some dead, some alive. She discusses the permanance of lost loved ones in the lives of those left behind: "Les morts ne meurent jamais, ils demeurent; le deuil n'est jamais fait et on n'atteint jamais le fond originel des choses" (Delvaux 102). [The dead never die, they remain; bereavement is never done and one never reaches the root of things.] Yan-Zi's death, like those of Zoulikha's and Djebar's other spectral characters, is not a final parting, and mother and daughter remain in one another's conscience due to the bond they share.

As the spirit of Yan-Zi observes funeral preparations, the funeral itself, and the dinner following the ceremony, she comments on various members of her family and how her death has affected them:

> Grand-mère et maman, ces deux femmes qui se détestent depuis tant d'années à cause de moi, vont donc pleurer ensemble devant ma tombe. Je veux que maman perde ses larmes, beaucoup de larmes, comme elle a perdu son sang le jour de ma naissance. C'est le prix qu'une mère doit payer. Quant à grand-mère, elle a payé cher son propre enfant. (IG 36)

> [Grandmother and Mom, these two women who have hated one another for so many years because of me, are going to cry together in front of my tomb. I want Mom to lose her tears, a lot of tears, like she lost her blood the day of my birth. It's the price that a mother must pay. As for Grandmother, she paid dearly for her own child.]

The contentious relationship between mother and grandmother represents their internalization of discourse on patriarchal and symbolic violence. The consistently negative interaction between Yan-Zi's mother and grandmother reflects symbolic violence in that these two women constantly want to inflict suffering on the other. It is a relationship that functions poorly on all levels. They reproduce symbolic violence for their daughter and granddaughter through continual expression of their strong dislike for one another, displayed in their arguments and their need to harshly criticize the other. The grandmother, for example, says to Yan-Zi:

> Le plus grand tort de ton père, commençait-elle ainsi en l'absence de maman, c'est d'avoir épousé une femme aux cheveux imprésentables; on dit que la qualité de la chevelure reflète celle de la personne. Ce

disant, grand-mère prenait le ton de ceux qui se croyaient d'une race meilleure et qui sentaient leur supériorité piétinée par des créatures médiocres. (IG 38)

["Your father's biggest error," she thus began in Mom's absence, "it's having married a woman with unpresentable hair; they say that the quality of the hair reflects that of the person." Saying this, Grandmother was taking the tone of those who believe themselves to be of a better race and who sensed their superiority stomped on by mediocre creatures].

Although Yan-Zi does not participate in the horrible relationship between mother and mother-in-law, she reproduces the negative schema in wishing to inflict emotional pain on her mother by committing suicide. Her tone is as harsh if not harsher than that employed by her mother and grandmother when she declares: "Je brûlais d'envie de voir maman souffrir à la vue de mon cadavre. Souffrir jusqu'à vomir son sang. Une douleur inconsolable" (IG 18). [I was burning to see Mom suffer at the sight of my cadaver. To suffer until she vomited her blood. An inconsolable pain.] This family most definitely functions within a matriarchal system, that is to say, one in which women hold power. Yet their behavior reinforces a system of control that seeks to repress women. Yan-Zi, like her mother and grandmother before her, has internalized patriarchal violence. In attempting to break away from her mother, she only succeeds in further implicating herself in the contentious and unpleasant matrilineal structure that dominates family life. She is no longer a simple victim of symbolic and patriarchal violence, but also a perpetuator of that violence which so inhibited her before her suicide. In consciously seeking to inflict emotional pain and suffering on her mother, Yan-Zi becomes an active participant in the negative cycle of patriarchal violence she witnessed between her mother and grandmother.

Death is not the peaceful refuge Yan-Zi had hoped it would be, nor does her family suffer as much as she had expected. Life goes on without Yan-Zi, a fact that her spirit has difficulty accepting. The longer she is dead, the harder it is for her to connect to the human plane, but one moment she sees members of her family processing together, and she realizes that they are celebrating the national holiday: "Tout peut arriver ce jour-là. . . . on mange de son mieux, on signe des contrats, on se marie, on fait l'amour ou l'on tue. Le sang coule librement quand le corps se détend. . . . Ce jour-là plus que les autres, on vit. Et on est heureux" (IG 94). [Anything can happen on that day. . . . People eat well, sign contracts, get married, make love, or kill. Blood flows freely when the body relaxes. . . . This day more than others, people live. And they are happy.] Her death does not mark the end of family life but rather a moment where aspects of family life and dynamics change drastically. Yan-Zi is no longer an active participant in daily family routines, and after her funeral, as her mother prepares tea for her father, Yan-Zi realizes that she will never again partake in this family ritual: "Maman vient fermer la porte. Je décide de rester dehors" (IG 66). [Mom comes to close the door. I decide to stay outside.] The gesture of remaining outside represents her recognition of the changing nature of family life and her inability to participate in that structure.

In *L'Ingratitude*, Yan-Zi reveals other rites and traditions. The figure of Seigneur Nilou is often mentioned by Yan-Zi's spirit, who has yet to find peace. Everything she knows about Seigneur Nilou comes from her grandmother's stories. He controls the world, deciding where and when each human being will be born and die, how each soul will be punished, and in what form the soul will return to Earth:

> Il s'occuperait de moi, ce tyran de l'univers Yin, [24] cette autre maman qui rendrait ma mort insupportable. Il se soucierait de nous faire naître, mourir, puis renaître, remourir, comme les insectes, comme n'importe quoi. Il ferait ce que maman ne pourra plus faire, c'est-à-dire qu'il se chargerait de me discipliner, de me punir en m'envoyant dans le monde des animaux domestiques, afin de m'inculquer davantage de sagesse. (IG 93)

> [He would take care of me, this tyrant of the Yin universe, this other mom who would make my death unbearable. He would take care to make us be born, die, then reborn, redie, like insects, like anything. He would do what Mom will never be able to do anymore, that's to say he would take it upon himself to discipline me, to punish me by sending me to the world of domestic animals, so as to further instill wisdom in me.]

This god-like figure does not conform to Christianity's perception of a benevolent god. Rather, Yan-Zi anticipates another authority figure, another *mother*, who will punish her for her wrongdoings. Upon her death, the narrator expects to be met by Seigneur Nilou, but "Il n'est pas là, ce Seigneur Nilou. Il aurait dû venir me chercher, noter quelque chose dans son cahier et me conduire dans son royaume" (IG 92). [He is not there, this Seigneur Nilou. He should have come to find me, mark something in his notebook and lead me to his kingdom.] As she waits for him, she is doomed to float in a vague and indefinable space between her earthly existence and the heavenly one she anxiously awaits. She has not succeeded in fully detaching herself from the human plane that was, for her, dominated by her mother. Nor has she been able to attach herself to the heavenly refuge she seeks, one that she expects to be run by Seigneur Nilou. Much as freedom from her mother has proven to be an illusion, so too has the existence of the afterlife she had hoped to attain.

Chen includes cultural references that indicate the Chinese descent of the narrator and her family, such as an allusion to President Mao (IG 54) and the names of characters (*Yan-Zi, Chun, Hong-Qi*). These indications are relevant to the unfolding of the story in that they remind the reader of the narrator's origins, suggest the restrictive environment in which she finds herself, and indicate the narrator's ambivalence towards China. Nevertheless, Chen creates a "placeless" city, a reflection of global urbanism, which could be almost any fairly large city with a Chinese community. We know that Yan-Zi's father is a professor, but the name of his university is never mentioned. The park Yan-Zi visits does not have a name. Aside from le Restaurant Bonheur that Yan-Zi frequents, Chen provides very few geographical markers. One reference that indicates the story probably takes place in China is an observation by the mother: "Il est trop dangereux de traiter de politique dans ce pays, déclarait-elle, on ne vit pas en Amérique" (IG 27). [It's too dangerous to discuss politics in this country, she declared, we don't live in America.] In spite of this one specific allusion, Chen creates a fairly anonymous setting and family that could be almost any middle-class Chinese family. Yan-Zi's tortured existence, both in life and death, is made universal by the lack of geographical references and sparse use of characters' names.[25] Not only does Yan-Zi's family seem to live in a "placeless" place, they are also presented as anonymous figures. The reader senses that the narrator and her family could be from anywhere and could blend into almost any urban community. Simon Harel views migrant literature's anonymous literary places as a refusal by authors to situate themselves in a specific space: "L'écriture du hors-lieu est aussi un projet qui réfute toutes les tentatives de marginalisation rassurante, d'exotisme convenu qui caractériseraient l'écriture migrante" (145–146). [Writing of "placelessness" is also a project that refutes all attempts of reassuring marginalization, of accepted exoticism that characterized migrant literature.] In her depiction of Yan-Zi's "place-less" spaces, Chen thus prevents the reader from making assumptions in regards to the narrator's surroundings. Rather, one has no choice but to focus on the spectral narrator's detailed chronicle of her miserable life and unfulfilling afterlife.

L'Ingratitude is not transcultural in the geopolitical sense of the word as are La Femme sans sépulture by Assia Djebar and Des rêves et des assassins by Malika Mokeddem, but the generational clashes manifested in the novel represent the meeting of two cultures: that of the adult daughter who embraces the ways of modern society and that of the mother who anchors herself to Chinese tradition and familial expectations, as dictated by Confucian philosophy. The restrictions imposed on the narrator by her mother concerning dating and marriage are the cause of much tension and heartache in the novel. Although Yan-Zi was a young career woman and experienced certain aspects of independence, her mother demanded that she observe tradition in dating and courting rituals, going so far as to insist upon choosing her daughter's future husband and monitoring her daughter's daily comings and goings. Yan-Zi's rejection of her mother's Confucian vision of family ties creates the explosive dynamic that haunts her even in the afterlife.

At first glance, the afterlife may seem like just another "place" for the unsettled narrator, yet this is most definitely not the case. Another trans-cultural characteristic of the novel is Chen's treatment of the space inhab-ited by Yan-Zi after her death. This foggy, indiscernible space also acts as a culture different from her own where her expectations are not met: "Depuis combien de temps déjà ai-je flotté ici? Je n'ai jamais vu un endroit si neutre, si privé de couleur, de senteur, de goût, de forme, de poids et de chaleur" (IG 129). [How long have I been floating here? I've never seen a place so neutral, so void of color, odor, smell, flavor, form, weight, and heat.] Yan-Zi's post-life lieu habité is another anonymous space difficult to distinguish from others due to its lack of landmarks and, in this case, other human beings or wandering souls. In Les passages obligés de l'écriture migrante, Harel refers to the description of espaces potentiels, or potential spaces. He explains that these imagined spaces allow the migrant writer to cope with the many traumas brought on by displacement and to express his or her fragmentary identity (Harel 149). One can examine Yan-Zi's afterlife through the prism of a potential space. In anticipating a more peaceful existence, Yan-Zi chose to take her life. Heaven, the imagined potential space she describes, distances her from her mother but does not provide comfort, refuge, and solace. On the contrary, the neutral, lifeless, and colorless space she occupies after her death highlights her solitude and unresolved inner conflicts. We cannot go so far as to say that Yan-Zi is homesick for her former life and her mother, but death and the afterlife challenge her in ways she had not anticipated, creating a sort of cultural shock. The afterlife does not meet her expectations, as she is still lonely, unsettled, and, most importantly, not able to cut herself off from her mother.

L'Ingratitude presents stark and disturbing mother-daughter conflicts that result from the inability of the two women to accept the other's wishes. Both women have internalized a discourse on patriarchal violence, and both women therefore seek to harm and inhibit the other. Yan-Zi and her mother are unwilling, and it would seem *unable* to achieve the entwinements described by Welsch. Their transcultural experience proves to be a very unhappy one. The nameless mother figure, both before and after her daughter's death, serves to impose and reinforce restraints placed upon her daughter.

In each of these three novels, the physical absence and death of a family member is the result of a different traumatic event, reminding us that transculturality is not always a fulfilling experience. For Zoulikha, a war of liberation separates her from her children. Keltoum's disappearance and eventual death in France stem from her husband's decision to take a second wife. Yan-Zi chooses to detach herself from her mother's oppressive influence by committing suicide. In death, each character's transcultural experience is emphasized through propagation of stories, as is the case with Zoulikha and Keltoum, or in examination of the afterlife as a transcultural space, as is Yan-Zi's experience in *L'Ingratitude*.

This chapter has demonstrated links that exist between different literary mothers and daughters from across the Francophone world. Evolving in transcultural contexts on different continents, their stories testify to the creative potential that life in diverse societies can offer to women. The hardships they face, including language and cultural barriers, color their interpersonal interactions and can serve to encourage introspection and creation. From these women's troubling circumstances, creative works often emerge, revealing frustration, transformation, and hope. Whereas this chapter focused on the transcultural interactions or lack thereof in the selected works, the following chapter will examine the importance of specific rural, urban, and mental spaces that contribute to women's creative lives.

NOTES

1. See Lori Saint-Martin's article in which she discusses the particularities of literature written by women. Lori Saint-Martin, "Le Nom de la mère: Le Rapport mère-fille comme constante de l'écriture au féminine."

2. It may be taken for granted by postmodern theory that gender lines are indistinct, yet that does not translate in many Third World literatures. Francophone literature exemplifies this fact. Not only are many Francophone societies highly misogynist, even more are homophobic, as pointed out by Maryse Condé in *Traversée de la Mangrove*.

3. Exceptions include Trinh, Spivak, and Lionnet, who each examine gender issues in their work.

4. In her 1976 study on motherhood, *Of Woman Born*, Adrienne Rich describes the institution of motherhood as one created by men in order to control women. While this work is not central to the present study, it has influenced the anthropological, sociological, and literary studies of mothers, their relationships with their children, and their roles in society. Rich's distinction between "institution" and "experience" is still employed in such studies.

5. Men can most definitely serve as mother figures, yet this is rarely seen in a Francophone context due to the tradition of male chauvinism in these cultures. One example of a novel where men serve as mother figures is *Traversée de la Mangrove* by Maryse Condé. In this novel, fathers who steal their children from their mothers end up acting as both mother and father for these children.

6. Rejecting motherhood is also a strong way for a woman to assert herself. One example of this is Simone de Beauvoir's refusal of motherhood as a way to free herself from what she perceives as a physical and societal handicap experienced by women. In *Parity of the Sexes*, Sylviane Agacinski offers sharp criticism of de Beauvoir's rejection of woman's maternal function, seeing it as "an absurd denial of nature, of maternity, and of the feminine body in general" (42). Agacinski proposes that rather than alienate herself from her body and its natural functions, a woman should be aware of that which distinguishes her from men, capitalizing on her femininity to liberate herself from "historical and natural

alienation" (60). The differences between men and women therefore have the possibility of being viewed by women as enriching rather than debilitating.

7. In *L'Homme dominé*, Albert Memmi puts forth the argument that modern women like Simone de Beauvoir were not really free, insisting that she renounced her right to marriage and family in an effort to please Jean-Paul Sartre. He finds that her freedom was not complete: "Pour être libre efficacement, la femme doit être considérée comme femme: c'est-à-dire comme amante et mère. Pour libérer la femme, il faudra instaurer des rapports nouveaux dans les relations amoureuses et dans la maternité" (167). [To be effectively free, women must be considered as women: that is to say, as lover and mother. To free women, new relationships in romantic relationships and in motherhood must be established.] On a similar note, Pierre Bourdieu claims that masculine domination can be overcome only through a major societal change: "The relation of complicity that victims of symbolic domination grant to the dominant can only be broken through a radical transformation of the social conditions of production of the dispositions that lead the dominated to take the point of view of the dominant on the dominant and on themselves" (41–42).

8. Colette, for example, writes about pregnancy as deforming the woman's body and the pains of labor in the short story "Maternité." In *Le Deuxième sexe*, de Beauvoir encourages women to either not have children or to choose the time to conceive a child very carefully.

9. Yolanda Astarita Patterson offers a complete analysis of de Beauvoir's mother figures in *Simone de Beauvoir and the Demystification of Motherhood*.

10. As discussed in the first chapter, there is some disagreement as to whether it is men or women who serve as guardians of culture. The theoricians of Creoleness claim that the male *oraliturian* fulfills this role, while Condé perceives women as guardians of culture.

11. In the case of Schwarz-Bart and other female Antillean writers, for instance, father figures are not only overshadowed by mother figures but also are more or less absent from the lives of their wives and children. Fathers, grandfathers, and boyfriends are seldom mentioned, and men remain at the periphery of the women's lives. The predominance of matrifocal, or mother-focused, families in the French Caribbean is examined in Arlette Gautier's *Women from Guadeloupe and Martinique*.

12. The first chapter of this study made a case for the transcultural literature, including Moisan's labeling contemporary Quebecois literature as *transcultural*. Likewise, he has identified other categories of Quebecois literature, including the *intercultural*, representing societies in which different groups co-exist and one approaches the other, either integrating into that culture or transforming it (Moisan 14–17).

13. The authors did not translate Creole expressions in the text, and I have chosen to maintain that format in my translation, as not translating the Creole can be a way to "colonize" the Western reader.

14. See this chapter's earlier discussion on displacement and trauma under "Mother Figures and the Consequences of Transculturality."

15. Oliveira identifies the term *Savane* as originating from the native Taino tribe. It also evokes images of Africa for a Eurocentric reader.

16. *Quartier-mélo*—mixed neighborhood. This is inspired by the French expression *méli-mélo* which refers to a mess, a muddle, or a jumble. Savane Mulet's mixed population has a multitude of problems, including poverty, incest, and natural disasters.

17. In migrant literature, redefinition of homeland is common, as notions of territory and nation are less and less a focus for identity in a postmodern and global context. Also, the province of Quebec is not a nation-state but a nation defined by a common language and culture.

18. Farhoud includes a lexicon of proverbs at the end of the novel, in Arabic with the French translation. Gathering the proverbs in one place in the text reiterates their instructive nature.

19. The name *Myriam*, Arabic for *Mary*, is the Old Testament name that becomes *Mary* in the New Testament. The name means "bitter" or "rebellious." The allusion to rebellion could refer to the fact that Douina's daughter is the courageous figure who desires to give her mother a voice by telling the story of her life.

20. *La femme sans sépulture*—the woman without a sepulture. This refers to the fact that Zoulikha's body was never found and she never had a proper burial. The title *la Femme sans sépulture* does not explain the issue of maternal absence, but it alludes to a wandering of the unsettled spirit whose final resting place is unknown to her family.

21. *La Femme sans sépulture* was published in 2002, the fortieth anniversary of Algeria's independence from France, but the story is being told some twenty years after Zoulikha's disappearance.

22. Muslim tradition dictates that the deceased are to be buried within a day of death. Unbeknownst to Zoulikha's family, the heroine actually was buried by a young soldier.

23. In Djebar's novels, the dead often speak, as is the case in *Le blanc d'Algérie*, a book in which the narrator undertakes a dialogue with three deceased friends. The deceased are not dead, and through literature their voices survive. Authors' use of spectral narrators is examined in chapter 4.

24. Yan-Zi attributes unjust and severe behavior to her mother's Yin nature, that is to say, to the feminine side of her personality. She therefore attributes Yin dominance to any powerful figure. Jamieson explains Yin-Yang societies as ones

that display opposing characteristics that balance one another: "*Yang* is defined by a tendency toward male dominance, high redundancy, low entropy, complex and rigid hierarchy, competition, and strict orthodoxy focused on rules for behavior based on social rules. *Yin* is defined by a tendency toward greater egalitarianism and flexibility, more female participation, mechanisms to dampen competition and conflict, high entropy, low redundancy, and more emphasis on feeling, empathy, and spontaneity" (13). Yan-Zi's experience on Earth reflects no balance, dominated by a powerful mother figure who unwittingly subscribes to patriarchal violence.

25. *Yan-Zi*, the main character's name, is not used until page 53. Her parents' first and last names are never revealed, and she refers to her grandmother simply as "Grand-Mère."

3

PLACE AND SPACE

Nurturing Creative Friction

In our examination of mother figures, we have seen that transculturality favors diversity, insomuch as contact between individuals fosters personal transformation. Interpersonal interactions or lack thereof impact the ways in which women perform the act of mothering. The heroine in Djebar's *La Femme sans sépulture* can rely on other women to care for her children when she is absent (first due to war, and then after her death). Farhoud's Dounia, on the other hand, finds childrearing to be a solitary endeavor in Canada, where she doesn't speak the language and deals with an unstable husband. One's surroundings, both natural and manmade, are also a factor in formation of the mother figure living in a transcultural context. How is a mother's behavior influenced by her surroundings? How does she use her experiences in her environment to enrich her understanding of herself, her family, and her community?

As we shall see, different backdrops have varying effects on mother figures. A mother may seek to shelter herself from a contentious community yet reemerge for the benefit of her family. The seasons of women's lives are likened to natural phenomena, depicting both joy and tragedy. Movement to and through multiple national and domestic spaces make for solitary mothers who refuse attachment to the spaces they know. Just as significant are the non-physical, mental spaces of memory and creation in which mothers and daughters seek respite and comfort. Different surroundings thus prove to be of importance in the formation of maternal identities.

Before we consider literary mother figures and the various environments in which they function, we should remind ourselves of Anne Donadey's assertion that the concerns of women Francophone postcolonial writers often coincide with those of postcolonial theory.[1] In that vein, discussion of postcolonial theories on place and space serves to inform our examination of the diverse settings in which literary mothers function.[2] Literature also offers the opportunity to examine the notions of place, space, appropriation, and reappropriation of space in postcolonial societies. One only has to consider such well-known texts as *Cahier d'un retour au pays natal*[3] by Aimé Césaire, "Les Femmes d'Alger dans leur appartement" by Assia Djebar, and *Traversée de la Mangrove* by Maryse Condé to recognize the importance that space can hold for those in postcolonial areas.

Many critics, including Deleuze, Guattari, and Glissant, choose to play down the importance of *lieux habités*, or "occupied places." Rather, they favor the notions of deterritorialization and wandering as ways to form and express one's identity in a globalized, postcolonial world. Yet, as Simon Harel notes in *Les passages obligés de l'écriture migrante*, examination of place is necessary so as to better annunciate the realities of the exile experience (111). The commotion created by change of scenery and landscape is an important element in identity formation in postcolonial contexts. Moisan, too, supports consideration of place and displacement as a way to better assess postcolonial literature:

> Le déplacement dont il s'agit n'implique plus la question d'un ailleurs, d'un lieu à atteindre, de personnes à mettre en contact, de rapports conflictuels ou non lors de ces rencontres, mais d'efforts et d'effets plus profonds de l'ordre de la transposition, de la transmutation, voire de la transcription, tous ces termes en "trans" indiquant à la fois le passage et le changement d'un lieu, d'un état ou d'un moment à un autre. (208)

> [The displacement it involves no longer implies the question of an elsewhere, of a place to reach, of people to put in contact, of relationships that are conflictual or not during these meetings, but of deeper efforts and effects in the nature of transposition, transmutation, indeed transcription, all of these terms in "trans" indicating simultaneously

the passage and change of a place, of a state, or from one moment to another.]

Moisan argues that examination of Quebecois literature requires an understanding of the complex modes of displacement experienced by immigrants. A *here* and *elsewhere* dichotomy does not suffice to explain Canada's *littérature migrante*, nor does it do justice to the literature of other diasporas. Rather, Moisan underscores the movement and transformation that the displaced person encounters, both of which contribute to identity formation. As time passes, both people and places change. So, examining the role a specific place has in the representation of literary figures allows for a nuanced understanding of their development.

Several postcolonial critics have written on the challenges presented concerning the reappropriation of space from the oppressor and subsequent inhabitation of that space. Edward Said describes the "primacy of the geographical," indicating that strong connection to place manifests in response to European territory aggression during colonial times:

> If there is anything that radically distinguishes the imagination of anti-imperialism it is the primacy of the geographical in it. Imperialism after all is an act of geographical violence through which virtually every space in the world is explored, charted, and finally brought under control. For the native, the history of his or her colonial servitude is inaugurated by the loss to an outsider of the local place, whose concrete geographical identity must thereafter be searched for and somehow restored. ("Yeats and Decolonization" 77)

Said's assertions incite perplexing questions, all relating to the identities of postcolonial citizens: How is one to reappropriate that which was taken so long ago? Can and should the newly reappropriated space be transformed so as to erase remnants of colonial history? Who should have the right to inhabit that space? Finally, how does space evolve through time?

As discussed in the first chapter of this book, Edouard Glissant's *Poétique de la relation* is in part concerned with identity formation in a world where seemingly limitless contacts are possible between human beings of different races and ethnicities. Place plays a role in the evolution of personal identity, insomuch as travel and wandering serve to enrich identity. Glissant does not encourage one to foster his or her connection a real or imagined homeland but rather to seek the "Other" and create a placeless, relational, Creole identity. Reappropriation of territory is not a primary concern of Glissant's cultural theory, but the space that one inhabits in a given moment contributes greatly to the creative process and development of the individual. Exploration of a variety of geographical areas therefore encourages cultivation of a diverse, Creole self.[4]

Postcolonial literature can provide a middle ground between Said and Glissant's contrasting arguments. The texts examined in this chapter put forth a great variety of landscapes and domestic spaces, demonstrating different degrees of attachment *to* and relationships *with* space. Whereas Schwarz-Bart presents mother figures integrated into the landscape through metaphor, Pineau's literary mothers experience adversarial relationships with their unwelcoming, sometimes violent environments. In *Le Bonheur a la queue glissante*, Dounia is forced to adapt to numerous spaces throughout her life, so she easily detaches herself from different domestic spaces and landscapes. The mother in Ying Chen's *L'Ingratitude* is tied to patriarchal tradition and dominates family space to such a degree that her adult daughter eventually commits suicide to escape her mother's domination. In *Un plat de porc*, Mariotte's mother and grandmother exist only in the mental space Mariotte goes to as she tries to escape the unhappiness of her life in a French retirement home. Study of these literary mother figures will demonstrate varied relationships with the environments in which they raise their families.

Likewise, we will see that each setting fosters creativity on the part of mothers or daughters. While these women's experiences in transcultural societies include strife and trauma, these very societies inspire creative action. In *La Femme sans sépulture*, Zoulikah takes up arms in a quest for freedom, and in *L'espérance-macadam*, Eliette revisits her tragic childhood in order to mother a young victim of incest. Similar to these mother figures, each of the women we study allows her voice to emerge in spite of, and perhaps thanks to, her combative surroundings. They share over meals, through writing, and sometimes even in silence. The spaces they inhabit, physical and otherwise, nurture the creative friction needed for mothers and daughters to exercise their agency.

IDENTIFYING FEMININE SPACES

The notion of postcolonial space is not uniquely physical, as evidenced in Bhabha's theory of a Third Space of enunciation. We recall that this proposed space is a result of cultural hybridity and allows for a rereading of history and tradition so as to give a voice to the oppressed. Bhabha's description of space is vague and difficult to discern compared to Said and Glissant's explanations of postcolonial spaces. His proposed Third Space is in part influenced by the colonizer's discourse and traditions. Yet the oppressor is not supposed to have access to this space, as the Third Space seeks to subvert the colonizer's authority and influence over the colonized. Since domination of space involves control of power and knowledge, the Third Space of enunciation seeks to strip the oppressor of his power to silence the oppressed, thus breaking the bonds imposed by colonialism. Liberation is to be achieved through subversion of the oppressor's authority, creating hybrid individuals with the ability to express themselves in the ambivalent Third Space.[5]

Much as Bhabha's Third Space aims to situate itself outside the influence of the oppressor, expression of feminine spaces lingers outside the patriarchal realm.[6] Contemporary literary and cultural theory, whether or not influenced by postcolonialism, is replete with references to "feminine space." *Writing Women and Space*, edited by Alison Blunt and Gillian Rose, examines women and their relationships to community through different representations of space, including landscapes, war fronts, and suburbia. Although not in a Francophone context, *Writing Women and Space* provides many examples of spaces that can be considered specifically "feminine." Condé's *La parole des femmes*, as we saw in the second chapter, describes a Caribbean Francophone feminine literary space distinct from that of a masculine space in its treatment and representation of women's roles in a given society. That feminine space is expressed through a woman's life experiences and the roles she plays in society, including those of wife, single mother, and daughter. Natasha Dagenais's article "L'espace migrant/l'espace de la mémoire: *Le bonheur a la queue glissante* d'Abla Farhoud" analyses feminine postcolonial space in conjunction with life lived in exile. She argues that various spaces, including physical, geographic, symbolic, metaphoric, and imaginary ones, all play a role in the formation of the principal mother figure as well as in her ability to express her own exile experience (Dagenais 125).

The preceding examples go to show that postcolonial concepts of space are wide-ranging and diverse, represented geographically, through travel, through subversion of colonial power, or from a uniquely feminine perspective. There is not a unified expression of postcolonial space but rather an array of perceptions, each undoubtedly influenced by elements such as neocolonial discourse, postcolonial educational systems, meetings between individuals, and personal reflection. This chapter examines spaces that are simultaneously feminine and postcolonial and which serve to form the principal mother figure.

MATERNAL IDENTITIES AND THE NATURAL WORLD

When considering the role of nature in literature, one often thinks of pastoral scenes or of Romantic poets wandering through the woods, seeking inspiration in the landscape. Yet the role of the natural world is not always idyllic and comforting, as literature of the French Caribbean demonstrates. Eric Prieto's chapter "Landscaping Identity in Contemporary Caribbean Literature" calls attention to the "determinant role played by the landscape in shaping the character and identity of the populace," citing novels by Glissant, Chamoiseau, and Condé to underscore the central role of the landscape in Creole literature. Prieto briefly recalls the history of the islands, pointing out the fact that virtually no one can claim a privileged connection to the land,[7] and so "this absence of an originary bond—aggravated by the injustices of colonial history and the absurdities of its ideology—seems to have instilled in West Indian writers a particularly acute sensitivity to the landscape's power as a symbol of regional identity, but also to the unstable, ideological nature of all such symbols" (142). As Prieto explains, geographic landmarks help form and reinforce a group's Creole identity. The literature of the region reflects the inextricable link between people and the unpredictable natural world. Through literature, their relationship with their environment therefore manifests in both positive and negative representations, some of which will be explored in this chapter.

The study of people's relationship to and interaction with their surroundings calls to mind a field of study that has thrived in English departments in the last several years—that of ecocriticism. Ecocriticism "takes as its subject the interconnections between nature and culture, specifically the cultural artifacts of language and literature" (Nixon 234). It is a field that studies the relationship between literature and the physical environment, which, of course, can be composed of both natural and manmade landscapes. At first, ecocriticism was considered primarily as an offshoot of American studies and concentrated on the work of American literary figures such as Henry David Thoreau, Ralph Waldo Emerson, Aldo Leopold, and Annie Dillard (Nixon 234). Yet recent years have seen a wider application of its principles, taking into consideration diverse urban and rural environments, such as inner-city America or the environmental disasters brought on by development in rural India. Herbert Tucker pares the field down to its most basic principles: "Ecocriticism thus claims as its hermeneutic horizon nothing short of *the literal horizon itself, the finite environment*[8] that a reader or writer occupies thanks not just to culturally coded determinants but also to natural determinates that antedate these, and will outlast them" (qtd. Love 1). One of ecocriticism's central concerns is, understandably, the state of the environment, but as Tucker explains, the *literal horizon* and the *finite environment* that people know and see every day play an integral role in the unfolding of their lives. This holds true for any landscape or environment, whether one lives in a bustling city, a steamy tropical climate, or a rural village.

In his article "Environmentalism and Postcolonialism," Rob Nixon calls for a meeting of postcolonialism and ecocriticism, two schools of thought that don't often cross paths. According to Nixon, divisions exist because of inherent differences in philosophies of the two movements. He explains that while postcolonialism focuses on hybridity, ecocriticism often favors "discourses of purity," such as virgin wilderness or the preservation of "uncorrupted last great places" (235). Displacement and migration are important themes in postcolonialism, contrary to the literature of place that dominates ecocriticism (235).[9] Nixon encourages a meeting of the two groups, insisting that literary environmentalism should not be a uniquely American domain: "By integrating approaches from environmental and Black Atlantic studies,[10] we might help bridge the divide between the ecocritical study of America's minority literatures and the ecocritical study of postcolonial literatures, which remains extremely rudimentary" (244). Study of the novels of Simone Schwarz-Bart and Gisèle Pineau respond to Nixon's call to analyze postcolonial literature from an ecocritical perspective. Colonialism and postcolonialism have the potential to play a significant role in ecocritical studies because, as noted at the beginning of the chapter, possession of land is a central concern in postcolonial societies. Furthermore, both colonizer and colonized have an affinity for the same land, oftentimes both claiming it as their homeland.[11]

Pluie et vent sur Télumée Miracle and *L'espérance-macadam* demonstrate the tenuous relationship between the Creole people and their environment, showing the deep connection that exists between a mother and the landscape with which she is most familiar. The principal mother figures in these two novels remind us of Prieto's assertions in that the trajectories of the characters' lives depend in part on the capricious nature of their surroundings. The natural world and island landscapes can also provide a comforting sense of permanence in the midst of life's difficulties, which include physical abuse, abandonment, and poverty.

Pluie et vent recounts the hardships and joys experienced by four generations of the Lougandor women, from Minerve the former slave to the narrator Télumée, who carries on the family tradition of feminine strength and optimism in moments of sadness and adversity. The title of the novel itself, *Pluie et vent sur Télumée Miracle*, announces both the hardships (rain and wind) and the redemption (miracle) that contribute to the unfolding of Télumée's life. The book brings the reader's attention to politically and socially sensitive topics, including Guadeloupe's history of slavery and the resulting social stratification of modern times, as well as violence against women and the undesirable family structure that exists due to abandonment of mothers and children. While refusing to condemn any one group for Guadeloupean society's downfalls, Schwarz-Bart addresses the oftentimes unpleasant realities, making them known to the reader. Through the stories of Reine Sans Nom and Télumée, the reader is made aware not only of the negative effects of slavery and colonialism that permeate daily life but also of the beauty and richness of the Creole culture. Storytelling is presented as a means to preserve culture, as a family's history is passed down from one generation of women to another. Spirituality is expressed through an amalgam of traditions—Catholic practices intermingle with religious rituals brought from Africa and an inherent trust in feminine power, resulting in goddess-like women characters who draw on their well of strength to cultivate and preserve their culture.[12]

An essential element of the feminine spirituality cultivated by the Lougandor women is that of communion with nature, as evidenced in

Reine Sans Nom's creation story: "Au commencement était la terre, une terre toute parée, avec ses arbres et ses montagnes, son soleil et sa lune, ses fleuves, ses étoiles. Mais Dieu la trouva nue, et il la trouva vaine, sans ornement aucun, c'est pourquoi il l'habilla d'hommes" (PV 80). [In the beginning was the earth, an adorned earth, with its trees and its mountains, its sun and its moon, its rivers, its stars. But God found it naked, and he found it pointless, without any ornament, that's why he dressed it with men.] According to Reine Sans Nom's Bible-like creation story, man and nature have been interconnected from the genesis of human existence. Human beings, placed on the earth to make it more interesting and colorful, use their innate powers of perception to mold their own image of the earth. She explains that one evil man from Fond Zombi fails to appreciate the beauty which surrounds him and therefore creates negativity: "Puisque les hommes n'étaient pas bons, les fleurs n'étaient pas belles, la musique de la rivière n'était qu'un coassement de crapauds. Il avait des terres, une belle maison de pierre que les cyclones ne pouvaient renverser, et il jetait sur tout cela un regard de dégoût" (PV 80–81). [Since men weren't good, the flowers weren't beautiful, the music from the river was only a croaking of toads. There were lands, a beautiful stone house that cyclones couldn't tip over, and he looked upon that with disdain.] The women of *Pluie et vent*, unlike the evil man in Reine Sans Nom's tale, choose to cultivate their relationship with the earth, accentuating the natural splendor that makes life bearable. Their stories and proverbs are sprinkled with references to the landscape, resulting in a text saturated with images of mountains, rivers, vegetation, and animals. The ideas of the *literal horizon* and *finite environment* referenced earlier in the chapter are fully pertinent to Reine Sans Nom and Télumée. The Lougandor women are keenly aware of their horizon and its role as backdrop to their lives and witness to their dramas.

Reine Sans Nom and Télumée know elation and unhappiness, as the reader is reminded with this proverb: "La femme qui a ri est celle-là même qui va pleurer, et c'est pourquoi on sait déjà, à la façon dont une femme est heureuse, quel maintien elle aura devant l'adversité" (PV 157). [The woman who has laughed is the same one who will cry, that is why we already know, by how a woman is happy, what strength she'll have when facing adversity.] The ups and downs they experience, including abandonment, death, and poverty, are always accompanied by the permanence of their natural surroundings. The island's landscape joins the residents of Fond Zombi to one another, creating and reinforcing a sense of community. Shortly after Télumée leaves her grandmother's home to start a life with Elie, she feels that an invisible force seems to be "knitting itself" around her home. Reine Sans Nom explains to her: "Tu le vois, les cases ne sont rien sans les fils qui les relient les unes aux autres, et ce que tu perçois l'après-midi sous ton arbre n'est rien d'autre qu'un fil, celui que tisse le village et qu'il lance jusqu'à toi, ta case" (PV 131). [You see, these huts are nothing without the threads that bind them to one another, and what you see in the afternoon under your tree is nothing other than a thread, the one that weaves the village and that it projects to you, to your hut.] One of the threads that joins Télumée to the other villagers is the landscape that acts as a common denominator between them.

References to nature and natural phenomena paint characters who maintain a close connection to their environment, oftentimes going so far as to directly associate woman to natural elements. Yet this environment is also hostile. In her article "Créolité and the Feminine Text in Simone Schwarz-Bart," Karen Smyley Wallace notes the extended metaphor of a woman's life as water: "Often the phases of a woman's life are referred to as 'les eaux de ma vie' (46) [the waters of my life], as she, symbolized by 'la barque enlisée' (26) [the stuck boat] launched upon these waters. At all times a woman must learn to navigate successfully on these waters to be prepared to face the constant currents of life itself" (556). Wallace also notes the "fusion" between woman and land, citing the following images in which the woman becomes: "basilier rouge" [red heliconia],[13] "peau d'acajou" [mahogany skin], "un fétu de paille sèche" [a wisp of dried straw], and "une gousse de vanille" [a vanilla bean] (556). As Wallace explains, these associations weave a text that is both feminine and Creole.

In a culture that favors orality and storytelling, one employs similes, metaphors, and proverbs to facilitate understanding, foster memory, and convey emotion. In "Oralité et écriture dans Pluie et vent sur Télumée Miracle," Nathalie Buchet Rogers enumerates some of the many functions of proverbs in the novel, revealing the tension between oral and written culture (435), the use of proverbs as a way to teach a lesson in few words (437), and as a way to contemplate the meaning of life (438). Rogers also notes the abundance of proverbs in Pluie et vent, both from African and French sources. She explains that the proverbs have been modified to suit specific situations: "Ils existent sous forme interrogative, négative, abstraite ou personalisée, et ne tirent leur signification que du contexte" (436–437). [They exist in interrogative, negative, abstract, or personalized form, and their meaning is pulled only from context.] The incorporation of traditionally French proverbs, undoubtedly familiar to the French reader, represents a subversion of the colonizer's own language, not only turning the voice of the white man against him but also breathing life into faded expressions that had lost their original meaning (Rogers 436). Rogers uses the example of Amboise's proverb to relay the following judgment of Europeans: "[Les blancs sont] 'des bouches qui se gavent de malheur, des vessies crevées qui se sont érigées en lanternes pour éclairer le monde'" (PV 223). [{Whites are} "mouths that stuff themselves with unhappiness, flat bladders that inflated themselves into lanterns to illuminate the world."] She explains that the harsh evaluation of the oppressor comes from the French proverb "prendre des vessies pour des lanternes" ("Oralité" 436). [use bladders as lanterns.] Although Amboise echoes the original French saying, he turns the words in such a way so as to criticize the oppressor with images from French culture. This displays both an understanding and subtle rejection of the colonizer's ways.

Rogers also observes that Schwarz-Bart's proverbs bind the characters to the landscape ("Oralité" 438). For instance, when Reine Sans Nom loses a daughter to a fire, her emotional spiral is likened to a fallen leaf decaying in a pond: "La feuille tombée dans la mare ne pourrit pas le jour même de sa chute, et la tristesse de Toussine[14] ne fit qu'empirer avec le temps, justifiant toutes les mauvaises présages" (PV 27). [The fallen leaf on the pond does not rot the day of its fall, and Toussine's sadness only got worse with time, justifying all the bad premonitions.] Her emotional state mirrors a natural occurrence, and the reader will likely retain the poignant image of the leaf decaying in the pond as well as the association to Reine Sans Nom. Another metaphor referring to that difficult time alludes to the inner strength for which the Lougandor women are known:

> Ils songeaient à la Toussine d'autrefois, celle en haillons, et puis la comparaient avec celle d'aujourd'hui qui n'était pas une femme, car qu'est-ce qu'une femme ? . . . un néant, disaient-ils, tandis que Toussine était tout au contraire un morceau de monde, un pays tout entier, un panache de négresse, la barque, la voile et le vent, car elle ne s'était pas habituée au malheur. (PV 29)

[They thought about the Toussine from before, the one in tatters, and then compared her to the one of today who wasn't a woman, for what is a woman? . . . a void, they said, whereas Toussine was, to the contrary, a piece of the world, a country upon herself, a spirit of black woman, the boat, the sail and the wind, for she was not used to unhappiness.]

The images of her as *a piece of the world, a country upon herself, a ship*, and *the wind* make Reine Sans Nom a truly exceptional figure who refuses to be defeated by the tragedies she faces. These kinds of metaphors, as Wallace notes, place the woman in her environment, demonstrating her interconnectedness with her surroundings. Additionally, these steadfast images are used to help ease the suffering inflicted by slavery's heritage and by poverty. They underscore Reine Sans Nom's will to persevere and thus project hope. It is worth noting that *Pluie et vent* does not attempt to explain the reasons for suffering, nor does the novel offer solutions. However, descriptions of the connections between human beings and nature is one way in which the characters are able to face painful situations and then carry on.

The previous examples show that suffering is a shared experience, which Schwarz-Bart relates in part through natural images. Reine Sans Nom also employs rich images to relate stories about acceptance of others. When Victoire leaves Télumée to be raised by her grandmother, many criticize her actions. Reine Sans Nom, aware of her daughter's shortcomings as a mother, refrains from judging Victoire: "Mes amis, la vie n'est pas une soupe grasse et pour bien longtemps encore, les hommes connaîtront même lune et même soleil, même tourments d'amour" (PV 46–47). [My friends, life isn't a fatty soup and for a long time to come, men will know the same moon and sun, the same torments of love.] In this instance, Reine Sans Nom exploits elements from nature to demonstrate the senselessness in rebuking others. The moon and sun are images that remind Reine Sans Nom's audience of the commonalities of humanity. Her dependence on concrete images as a way to reinforce her teachings is a cultural statement opposed to Western Cartesian logic. In Cartesian tradition, perception and the five senses are unreliable tools in one's search of knowledge. It is only through reason that one attains knowledge, which in turn is represented through one's ideas. Schwarz-Bart's use of common natural images to demonstrate a truth is both a significant break from Western thought and an assertion of a Creole view of a human being's relationship with his or her surroundings.

IN THE GARDEN: STRENGTH AND JOY

The metaphors employed in *Pluie et vent*, brimming with strong associations between woman and nature, are part of what Jacques Le Marinel refers to as the quest for an *espace identitaire*, or identitary space.[15] Such a space allows for personal evolution in spite of the alienation one experiences in a racist society. Reine Sans Nom and Télumée do not isolate themselves from their community, but as exceptionally strong characters, they grow in a separate space that allows them to overcome some of the obstacles created by slavery and economic hardship. Their strong ties with nature show an effort to foster a Creole culture far from the reaches of the misery left by colonialism (Le Marinel 49). One of the notable elements of the search *for* and realization *of* an espace identitaire is the garden cultivated by Reine Sans Nom, and after her death, by Télumée. In this novel, grandmother and granddaughter each construct a feminine universe, one devoid of patriarchal influence, in the garden:

> Si on m'en donnait le pouvoir, c'est ici même en Guadeloupe, que je choisirais de renaître, souffrir et mourir. . . . Mais je ne suis pas venue sur terre pour soupeser toute la tristesse du monde. A cela, je préfère rêver, encore et encore, debout au milieu de mon jardin, comme le font toutes les vieilles de mon âge, jusqu'à ce que la mort me prenne dans mon rêve, avec toute ma joie. (PV 11)

> [If given the power, it's here in Guadeloupe that I would choose to be reborn, suffer, and die. . . . But I did not come to earth to handle all the sadness of the world. Instead of that, I prefer to dream, again and again, standing up in my garden, like all the old ladies my age, until death takes me in my dream, with all my joy.]

This passage, taken from the first page of the novel, establishes the garden as Télumée's domain, as her kingdom from where she will unravel her story. This is significant, as she begins her story from a place of strength, the reader imagining her taking a tree-like stance in that feminine space. The garden is central to Télumée's identity, as it is where her grandmother's stories were woven and passed on to her. This espace identitaire provides comfort and a sense of permanence without denying the suffering of the Lougandor women. Although a space of freedom and creation for Télumée, her garden does not represent an idealized domain that erases the hardships she and her ancestors have known.

Rather than use her garden as an escape from oppression and tragedy, Télumée instead is able to experience joy in that space, all while acknowledging suffering and the inevitable end of life. Sarah Phillips Casteel identifies the Caribbean garden as an "aid in the process of reimagining place" (12). Contrary to the poetic of wandering that Glissant would later formulate in *Poétique de la relation*, Schwarz-Bart's sense of place reinforces the value of rootedness as a way to understand and enunciate the self.[16]

The setting of *Pluie et vent*, expressed through description of landscape and numerous metaphors associating the mother to the natural world, proves to be a nurturing space where mothers cultivate courage and self-worth. Gisèle Pineau's *L'espérance-macadam* shares several characteristics with *Pluie et vent*, as remarked by Chantal Kalisa:

> The two novels both highlight the relationships between women and space, more specifically, the ways in which women achieve self-realization within such an ambiguous site where deterritorialized, and transplanted people attempt to *se change[r] en autre chose*. (108) [change oneself in to something else]

Although transformation is a theme that runs through both novels, Pineau paints a harsher, more violent picture of the Guadeloupean climate and the way it affects mother figures. Whereas Scwharz-Bart's mother figures find reassurance in the landscape used to illustrate their stories, Pineau's vision of nature is one that is more combative, oftentimes seeming to pit itself against the inhabitants of Savane Mulet. Our examination of this novel will nonetheless demonstrate the existence of certain associations between humans and landscape in *L'espérance-macadam*. Although that relationship is at times portrayed as adversarial, there is nevertheless a dependence on their island and its unpredictable meteorological behavior.

NATURAL DISASTER: CHAOS AND CLEANSING

Eliette, a childless widow, makes her home in the town, remaining on the fringes of society and at times sharing her reflections on her neighbors and life in the village. Although much of the story is told by a third person omniscient narrator, Eliette's first person interventions inform the reader of Eliette's loneliness, her yearning for a child, and her memories of growing up in Savane Mulet.[17] The town has always had the reputation as a place of *mauvaiseté*, or "badness" (EM 8), as a feeling of wickedness pervades life in the area.[18] Initially settled by Eliette's stepfather, Savane Mulet always made Eliette's mother uncomfortable, who claimed it was hell on earth due to the violent cyclones (EM 23). The combination of nature's brutality and humankind's subversive behavior makes for a seemingly miserable existence in Savane Mulet, yet Pineau succeeds in creating a place where hope does not die.

Although Eliette has always wanted a child, she was never able to conceive, and so she has spent her life as a "childless mother,"[19] hoping against hope for a child and even visiting a Haitian fortune-teller who swore that she saw Eliette with a daughter (EM 9). Her visit to the fortune-teller and the thought that she may mother a child stays with Eliette into her old age, acting as a ray of hope in the lonely circumstances of her life.

Eliette and the other citizens of Savane Mulet lead lives with the constant threat of natural disasters such as cyclones. Tales of past tragedies, including the cyclone of 1928 and the current destruction left in the wake of another hurricane,[20] paint a people and a town repeatedly ravaged by Mother Nature's aggressions. The cyclone also acts as an allegory, representing not only its inherent destructive energy, but also as a rapist, both of the landscape and of the people. The debilitating effects of incestual rape experienced both by Eliette and Angela, the daughter she finally adopts in her old age, are equated to the raw power of a hurricane:

> C'était sa maman qui lui racontait toujours la nuit où le Cyclone avait chaviré et pilé la Guadeloupe. Elle criait ce cauchemar: "Le Passage de La Bête." Et, pour mieux embobiner l'histoire dans la mémoire d'Eliette, elle ne cessait de faire défiler le souvenir de la blessure à la tête et au ventre, le sang dans les draps, la grosse poutre tombée qui avait manqué fendre Eliette en deux parts, le vent entrant méchant, bourrant, calottant. (EM 93)

[It was her mother who always told her about the night when the Cyclone had shook and pillaged Guadeloupe. She cried out this nightmare: "The Passage of The Beast." And, so as to better embed the story in Eliette's memory, she didn't cease to parade the memory of the head and stomach injuries, the blood on the sheets, the huge fallen beam that had almost split Eliette in two, the mean wind entering, filling, slapping.]

In a close reading of *L'espérance-macadam*, "La Bête" simultaneously represents the father, the storm, and the lifelong emotional scars they leave on Eliette. She recalls little about that night, but throughout her life, her mother's incessant retelling of the story burns itself into Eliette's memory. The two evil, enigmatic forces, the father and the hurricane, leave her with unanswered questions alluded to throughout the novel. Why is Eliette sterile? Is the cyclone to blame, or the other *bête*, her father? Did that violent time damage her for life, or in her old age will she be able to let go of the painful images instilled in her by her mother's repeated recounting of those stories? The cyclone of 1928 and the father are intertwined in her memory, and therefore in the novel, as she shares the story of her life.[21]

The hurricane, or rather, the *possibility* of a hurricane, is an obsessive, omnipresent threat in Savane Mulet, so much that stories about these storms have become part of the internal landscape of the people. In her article "Cyclone Culture and the Paysage Pineaulien," Elizabeth Walcott-Hackshaw refers to this as a "cyclone culture" in which lore and legends form around stories of past hurricanes and in anticipation of future ones (111). The first paragraph of *L'esperance-macadam*, for instance, describes the ruins left by a hurricane: "Restait rien de bon. Que des immondices. Y avait pas même une planche debout, une tôle en place" (EM 7). [Nothing good left. Only garbage. Not even a board standing, a piece of sheet metal in place.] Destruction is reflected in the language, the choppy rhythm and dropped words indicating the damage caused by the hurricane. Right from the beginning of the novel, the reader is surrounded by the destruction left by the storm, but in the midst of the bewildering images of suitcases hanging from the sky and mattresses strewn about, he or she has no geographic or temporal clues to indicate the setting or time period in which the story will unfold. Throughout the book, temporal indications are lacking, as the reader jumps from storm to storm and decade to decade. The images of destruction and fragmentary language set the tone for the forthcoming story, which sheds light on both the natural and human destruction to which the Guadeloupean people are submitted.

Images of devastation and sadness saturate the pages of *L'espérance-macadam*, but these startling descriptions are complemented by a vague, ever-present hope expressed at different points in this book. In the first paragraph of the book, one that is filled with images of the violence inflicted upon Savane Mulet, images of optimism linger with those of hate and despair: "Odeurs de l'amour et des femmes en chaleur, odeur du pain chaud de Sonel, . . . Parfum de rêves d'or, espoir d'enfantement . . . Et aussi, relents des bouches amères de jalousie crachant des prières au suppôts de Satan" (EM 7). [Odors of love and of women in heat, odor of Sonel's warm bread, . . . Perfume of golden dreams, hope of giving birth . . . And also, the stench of bitter mouths of jealousy spitting prayers to Satan's sidekicks.] The calming and reassuring scenes of writers such as Colette and Schwarz-Bart are absent, but dreams and hope juxtapose the surplus of negative images that meet the reader in the first lines of the story. Hope is never totally quashed by all that is evil.

Hope also weaves itself into the story through the use of allegorization, creating a destabilizing format akin to the complicated structure of Colette's *La Naissance du jour*, where different voices and forms of text are pieced together to tell a story. In *L'espérance-macadam*, the narrator explains that Angela's mother Rosette gives her daughter lengthy, story-like dictations in the afternoons. These are interspersed throughout the book, often without introduction, and set off in italics: "*Il se trouvait un jardin magique et magnifique de l'autre côté d'un pont . . . le travail n'avait pas la figure de l'esclavage, parce que la pluie et le soleil aimaient l'Espérance*" (EM 147). [*There was a magic and magnificent garden at the other side of the bridge . . . but work didn't have the face of slavery, because rain and sun loved Hope.*]

Hope, like the cyclone, is an allegory. In *L'espérance-macadam*, Pineau presents the two as opposing yet complimentary forces like the Chinese Yin-Yang symbol. The storm and hope are present, balancing one another yet also struggling to overtake the other. The cyclone never succeeds in destroying hope, and hope is eternally threatened by the possibility of a storm or other heartbreaking tragedy. In Angela's dictation, the allegory alludes to a time before slavery and racism, a period where there was optimism and justice, and when the land had not been destroyed by man and nature. The passage illustrates a criticism of history in a way that a child would be able to comprehend. In spite of the difficult life in Savane Mulet, one defined by poverty, violence against women, and crimes that go unpunished, there is a grain of optimism represented by *l'Espérance*.

The destruction brought by various storms is one of the central themes of the novel, but the startling violence of a storm can also act as a cathartic element, as we also see in *L'espérance-macadam*. Stories of the cyclone of 1928 and the events of that night have haunted Eliette throughout her life, and it is thanks to the arrival of another hurricane as well as the arrival of Angela into her home that she is finally able to come to terms with her sad past. The idea of mothering the young girl, also a victim of incest, and the need to protect her from the hurricane help Eliette in her own journey of emotional healing. Angela, too, sees the value of the oncoming storm as a cathartic tool, as shown in the following passage: "Angela fit un vœu et demanda au cyclone de nettoyer son corps au plus profond, de la remettre tout entière comme avant, au temps de l'innocence" (EM 207). [Angela made a wish and asked the cyclone to deeply clean her body, to make her whole again like before, in the time of innocence.] *L'espérance-macadam* ends with a series of beginnings—a new outlook on life for Eliette, a new home for Angela, and a new community responsibility to rebuild Savane Mulet.

One could say that Pineau's descriptions of the natural forces that play out on the island of Guadeloupe are more realistic than those of Schwarz-Bart. Walcott-Hackshaw points out, however, that one must keep in mind both the generational differences and distinctive literary styles of the two authors: Unlike earlier Guadeloupean writers such as Simone Schwarz-Bart and Maryse Condé, Pineau tackles questions of female sexuality and sexual violations against the female body in a more explicit, probing manner. Whereas Schwarz-Bart's language remains suggestive on these subjects, Pineau uses them as primary themes (EM 116). There are also a few important differences in the presentation of the characters that are worth mentioning. Although both writers present mothers who strive to overcome the difficulties they know as black women living in Guadeloupe, their problems are not identical, and nor are the ways they navigate them. Reine Sans Nom and Télumée each hold a privileged place in Fond Zombi as respected, mythical women who hold and share knowledge and history with others. Eliette has never been granted that status, nor has she sought to attain it. She has chosen to stay in the margins of society, emotionally and physically damaged from incest, while Schwarz-Bart's characters are constantly held up as examples within the context of their community.

All three of these figures are victims of violence, whether it be domestic, sexual, or the symbolic violence inherited from slavery and colonialism. Eliette is unique in that she is a victim of incest, a form of violence that debilitates her for most of her life. The violence she experienced as a child is primarily expressed through the allegory of the cyclone that also plagues the island, for the cyclone of 1928 coincides with her childhood rape. The contrasting natural images put forth by the two authors hold important similarities. First and foremost, through the act of storytelling the Caribbean landscape comes to parallel human emotion. Just as Schwarz-Bart represents female strength through metaphors of woman as earth and water, the emotional whirlwinds and traumatic moments experienced by Eliette are expressed through the allegory of cyclones. Second, in spite of its intimidating raw energy, nature can be a protective, purifying force that provides comfort or catharsis.

The works of Schwarz-Bart and Pineau show that natural surroundings can incite both calm and turmoil. Télumée, Reins Sans Nom, and Eliette articulate the significance that people often give to their surroundings, whether they are secure or combative. We have seen that familiar environments can provide sobering challenges to women. This is all the more true when they experience upheaval through displacement and changing backdrops.

SILENCE AND SHARING

In *Lettres parisiennes: Autopsie de l'exil*, Leïla Sebbar explains the place of exile in her life and writing: "[Exile] is the only place where I can enunciate the contradictions, the division . . . If I speak of exile, I speak also of cultural crossings; it is at these points of junction or of disjunction where I am, that I see, that I write" (qtd. in Orlando, *Nomadic Voices* 213). Sebbar identifies exile as a *place* which allows her to exist, perceive, and create. There is no question that the exile experience can be traumatic, but it can also embody a privileged space of expression. How might this inner "place" of exile contribute to a woman's vision of self and her understanding of her place in her home or community? Upon emerging from contemplation, how does she interact with others, and how does she elect to use the knowledge gleaned in exile?

Although it may seem counterintuitive, dynamic and diverse communities are often ones in which people feel alone. While isolation is often associated with loneliness, being cut off from others linguistically or culturally can allow for reflection and creation. In *Un plat de porc*, loneliness and a sense of detachment provide the impetus for Mariotte to begin recording her thoughts in her notebooks. Dounia, the narrator of *Le bonheur a la queue glissante*, also experiences interiority as an immigrant in Canada, where verbal communication serves as a barrier. This study has thus far highlighted the harshness of life in a transcultural environment, but we will also see that transculturality allows for mother figures to go within, reflect, and discover alternate modes of communication.

Spending a lifetime between Canada and Lebanon has allowed Dounia to compare ways of life: "Pour moi, ici ou là-bas, j'habiterais là-bas, puisqu'ils sont ici, c'est ici que je suis. La seule différence, c'est le climat. Plus de calme ici à cause de la neige, plus de joie là-bas à cause du soleil" (BQ 36). [For me, here or there, I would live there, since they're here, it's here that I am. The only difference is the climate. More calm here due to the snow, more joy there due to the sun.] She stays in Canada because it's there that she is surrounded by family. Although she insists on the similarities between the seemingly different countries, she does note a difference in climate. Canada's snow and long winters create a peace that she doesn't find in Lebanon—a peace that undoubtedly encourages reflection.

Compared to the rich description and personification of the natural world seen in Schwarz-Bart and Pineau, *Le Bonheur a la queue glissante* seems to lack landscape description. While other mother figures feel the need to describe and equate themselves to the landscape, Dounia possesses a detachment from the different backdrops she has known. She is able to adapt to change, but she does admit that snow and sun make for different sorts of existence. The decades she has spent in Canada, surrounded by snow, suggest a long-term and formative interiority that supports her inner place of exile. I posit that the extended quiet she experiences, due to both linguistic barriers and climate, enhances her understanding of complex human interactions.

Sharing stories through mediation of her grown daughter since she does not know how to read or write, Dounia expresses a hesitation to speak: "Quelquefois j'aimerais pouvoir parler, avec des mots. J'ai oublié, avec le temps" (BQ 15). [Sometimes I'd like to be able to speak, with words. I've forgotten, with time.] Dounia may have difficulty using words, yet those she chooses seem to be heard: "Elle me fait sentir que ce que je dis est important. Avec elle, j'ai l'impression d'être la reine mère" (BQ 21). [She makes me feel that what I say is important. With her, I feel like the Queen Mother.] Dounia understands that she is not limited to written and spoken modes of communication. Her dedication to her children and grandchildren is evident throughout the novel as she prepares meals for them: "Mes mots sont les branches de persil que je lave, que je trie, que je découpe, les poivrons et les courgettes que je vide pour mieux les farcir, les pommes de terre que j'épluche, les feuilles de vigne et les feuilles de chou que je roule" (BQ 14). [My words are the parsley stems I wash, I sort, I cut, the peppers and zucchini I empty to better stuff them, the potatoes I peel, the grape leaves and cabbage leaves I roll.] Food and meal preparation are a constant in Dounia's life, something consistent she has been able to carry with her through consecutive moves, from continent to continent. Dounia considers food as her primary form of expression since words often fail her: "Je ne suis pas très bonne en mots. Je ne sais pas parler. Je laisse la parole à Salim. Moi, je donne à manger"[22] (BQ 14). [I'm not very good with words. I don't know how to talk. I let Salim speak. Me, I feed people.] Clearly, allowing her husband to speak for her is a reflection of the patriarchal structure of her household and of the repression she has experienced in her often-troubled marriage.

Yet in attributing Dounia's quiet ways solely to patriarchal constraints, we ignore the nuances of family life as it is portrayed in the novel. At family gatherings, food is central. It brings people together, nourishes, and is thus a powerful tool in which this mother and grandmother transmits concern and love. Dounia is not the only silent member of the family. Her daughter Myriam is an educated author and divorced mother who displays an interiority that echoes that of her mother: "Dans les réunions de famille, elle est silencieuse comme moi. . . . Je ne la comprends pas toujours très bien. . . . De tous mes enfants, c'est elle que je sens la plus loin de moi et en même temps la plus proche" (BQ 24). [At family reunions, she is silent like me. . . . I don't always understand her very well. . . . Of all my children, it's her that I feel the farthest from me and at the same time the closest.] Dounia recognizes and identifies her daughter's *opaqueness*. They share a language, but she believes that education has changed her daughter, somehow made her harder to understand (BQ 25). In spite of the differences in education and experience, this mother-daughter pair connects through their mutual affinity for silence: "Myriam ne laisse entrer personne quand elle écrit. Sauf moi. Je suis si discrète qu'elle oublie que je suis là. Je ne lui parle jamais, elle non plus" (BQ 26). [Myriam doesn't let anyone enter when she writes. Except me. I am so discrete that she forgets I'm there. I never talk, neither does she.] Members of a noisy, talkative family, Dounia and Myriam find a way to share silence. Each one's need to pull back from spoken language and into a quiet, inner space is understood by the other. As she works her way through *Le Bonheur a la queue glissante*, the reader comes to understand that the novel is a product of this mother-daughter collaboration.

Dounia acknowledges and values the mental space she cultivates over the years, which gives her refuge from the activity of everyday life and helps her to cultivate understanding of herself and those she holds dear. Her inner landscape is an important one, but she is also conscious of her physical surroundings. In the first lines of the novel, she announces to her grown children: "Le jour où je ne pourrai plus me suffir à moi-même, mettez-moi dans un hospice pour vieillards" (BQ 9). [The day that I can no longer care for myself, put me in an old person's home.] This abrupt command, which serves as an introduction to the novel, announces a consideration of physical space that will weave itself throughout the story as Dounia recounts the various migrations her family has undergone throughout her lifetime, from her native village in Lebanon, to her husband's village, to Canada, back to Lebanon, and finally to settle once again in Canada. Dounia has occupied a multiplicity of spaces throughout her lifetime, each which has formed her. Dounia develops little attachment to domestic spaces, which in turn prevents these domestic *spaces* from becoming *places* endowed with sentimental value. She experiences shocking changes of scenery that profoundly affect her as a mother and wife. First, she leaves her native Lebanese village for that of her husband. A number of years later, she joins her husband in Canada with their children. They return to live in Beirut for a short while and then return to Canada definitively. In each country, they live in a number of different homes.

At one point in the book, Dounia reveals that her name means "universe" (BQ 95). The notion of space and the space that she inhabits is thus significant as she tells her story. This mother figure, although illiterate and often unsure of herself, nonetheless proves to be the force that holds her family together through numerous moves and difficult times. She is keenly aware of space, homes, and how her presence influences a given situation. This may be due to the fact that she has known so many different domestic spaces throughout her life: her father's home, her mother-in-law's home in Canada, and a series of rented apartments and houses, some shared with landlords. She has learned the importance of possessing one's own space, no matter how humble it may be: "A cette époque, j'ai compris qu'il vaut mieux vivre dans une mansarde à soi que dans le château d'un autre" (BQ 72). [At this time, I learned that it's better to live in one's own attic apartment than in the chateau of another.] However, Dounia expresses no attachment to the various houses she has lived in, claiming that one must be ready to adapt and learn:

> Pour moi, une maison est une maison. On y habite toute sa vie. Celle des parents d'abord, puis celle du mari qui devient notre maison si tout va bien avec le mari. Quand on change de pays, on doit changer aussi tout ce que l'on connaît sur la vie. On doit apprendre vite. Ca ne m'a jamais dérangée, au contraire, j'aime apprendre des choses nouvelles. (BQ 69)

> [For me, a house is a house. We live in one all our lives. That of the parents first, then that of the husband which becomes our house if all goes well with the husband. When one changes countries, one also changes everything she knows about life. We have to learn fast. That never bothered me, to the contrary, I like to learn new things.]

Dounia's attitude protects her from becoming attached to a certain space, as Télumée is to her garden. Although she is at times nostalgic for childhood and her native village, Dounia generally does not mourn lost space and former homes. "Her" spaces do not seem to transform in to loved places, teeming with memories and emotion. The familial and financial instability that she has known all her adult life has not given her the opportunity to become attached to the spaces she has occupied. "Home" is therefore represented by her family: "Mon pays, ce n'est pas le pays de mes ancêtres ni même le village de mon enfance, mon pays, c'est là où mes enfants sont heureux" (BQ 22). [My country, it's not the country of my ancestors or even my childhood village, my country, it's where my children are happy.]

Dounia has lived on different continents and in both rural and urban settings. Continual relocation has defined her adult life, unlike the Caribbean mothers we have seen whose surroundings forge a sense of permanence. Is there a landscape or a place that Douina claims as her own? She explains that relocation and displacement have provided her with different perspectives: "Emigrer, s'en aller, laisser derrière soi ce que l'on va se mettre à appeler *mon* soleil, *mon* eau, *mes* fruits, *mes* plantes, *mes* arbres, *mon* village. Quand on est dans son village natal, on ne dit pas *mon* soleil, on dit *le* soleil" (BQ 42). [Emigrate, depart, leave behind that which one will take to calling *my* sun, *my* water, *my* fruits, *my* plants, *my* trees, *my* village. When one is in his native village, one doesn't say *my* sun, one says *the* sun.] Memories of Dounia's village will always hold *her* sun, *her* fruits, and *her* water, but no space could be home without *her* family because of the numerous displacements she has undergone.

Throughout *Le bonheur a la queue glissante*, Dounia always returns to the idea of home and to the space she occupies. For instance, she remarks that in her old age it has become easier to occupy space: "Chez mes enfants, surtout chez ceux où je vais plus souvent, je suis comme chez moi. Maintenant que je suis vieille, partout c'est ma place" (BQ 77). [In my children's homes, especially the ones where I go the most often, I make myself at home. Now that I'm old, everywhere is my place.] The novel is sprinkled with references to space, evidence of Dounia's need to consider the spaces she has known. The ideas of *space*, *country*, and *home* are all fluid to her. She has and continues to inhabit a variety of spaces. She even anticipates the last space she intends on occupying before death, the hospice to which she refers several times throughout the book. She claims no country and makes a home wherever she must. *Her* landscape is therefore defined by the present moment.

A notable difference between Dounia and her Caribbean counterparts examined earlier in this chapter is that Dounia's horizon is mostly limited to the home—both her home and the homes of her children. The home is thus her primary landscape. Each of her landscapes, that is to say, each of her homes, is linked to specific family memories, most of them negative, since the novel critiques nostalgia for the homeland. Her childhood landscape is linked to the image of her orthodox priest father who did not feel the need to teach his daughter to read; the landscape of her newlywed years is marked by images of her husband's village; later years and travels demonstrate the vastness of the world; and in her old age her landscape is defined by interaction with family members, often taking place over a shared meal. Dounia's household is her domain—the space where she feels the most comfortable and in control. Yet the specific domestic space is much less important than the people who occupy that space. She does not come to know and understand the world through interaction with nature. Nor is she likened to natural elements from the landscape. Rather, movement and upheaval define this mother whose name signifies the universe—in a transcultural context. She achieves understanding and gains wisdom through those changes of country, language, scenery, and landscape. In spite of the many obstacles she encounters as an immigrant, Dounia is nonetheless an encompassing mother figure who demonstrates a great amount of resolve as she is able to detach herself from, and even denounce, different domestic spaces she has known.

MISERY AND SOLITUDE

In *Le Bonheur a la queue glissante*, Dounia's isolation is manifest, but she finds a measure of comfort in pulling away from chaotic family life. *Un plat de porc* also details the solitary life of an elderly woman, but Mariotte's existence is not brightened by enthusiastic grandchildren. Rather, she finds herself stuck in a French nursing home, with no family and very modest means. Given Mariotte's age and weakened physical condition, her mind provides her with the most practical way to reconnect to the people and places of her past. She has no daughter to recount her story. Instead, she documents her loneliness, anger, and desperation in a series of notebooks that she keeps hidden under her bed. While Mariotte's first notebook focuses on the misery of the retirement home and her reticence to remember her past, in the beginning of the second, she finally allows herself to rifle through her stack of personal belongings. She removes an envelope from the pile, conceals it from her companions, and goes to the restroom to examine its contents: the leaf of a philodendron plant from Martinique.[23] The leaf has preserved enough of its luster and lushness to calm Mariotte and remind her of home: "Longuement j'ai caressé la feuille gisante, du doigt, de l'ongle; sans parvenir à me défaire de son charme" (PP 45). [I caressed the limp leaf for a long time, with my finger, with my nail; without ever tiring of its charm.] This souvenir represents a pleasant union of present and past and triggers Mariotte's first jolting remembrance of childhood, where she encounters her domineering grandmother. Once the leaf unleashes images from her past, Mariotte fills her notebooks with a series of leaps between decades and continents.

As we saw earlier in this chapter, Dounia finds no need to romanticize the homeland. Likewise, Mariotte's imagined returns to her island are in no way idealized, as they remind her of the stark, difficult lives she and her family led in Martinique. Yet her notebooks reveal that the sadness of her childhood memories pale in comparison to the systematic oppression that occurs in the heterotopic space of the nursing home.[24]

In *Un plat de porc*, the space of Mariotte's retirement home functions as an isolated society whose members regularly inhibit their peers through use of symbolic violence. Pierre Bourdieu's book *Masculine Domination* details ways in which patriarchal societies maintain gender divisions, thus reinforcing masculine power in churches, governments, schools, and families. He employs the term *symbolic violence* to describe "a gentle violence, imperceptible and invisible even to its victims, exerted for the most part through the purely symbolic channels of communication and cognition, recognition, or even feeling" (Bourdieu 2). Mariotte's notebooks depict an elderly population that oppresses through verbal criticism, exclusion, and manipulation. Mariotte and the other residents are all witnesses to and recipients of this subtle, non-physical violence. In addition, they each seem to act as purveyors of symbolic violence, aiming to repress their peers and consequently maintaining the status quo of masculine domination within the walls of the home.

Catholic nuns are responsible for the care of Mariotte and her peers. Her account of life in the Catholic institution, however, is void of the affection and comfort that one might expect from those who serve as the face of the Catholic Church and transmitters of its messages. According to Mariotte, the nuns seem to be weighed down by their convictions, emptying bed pans day in and day out to demonstrate the purity of their souls (PP 20). In taking religious vows, they have committed to perpetuating the masculine social order so visibly maintained by the male hierarchy of the church that denies women the right to serve as priests. They are therefore contributors to their own oppression, as Bourdieu insists that victims of symbolic violence always are (40). In subscribing to the Catholic doctrines that exclude them from filling the same roles as men, the nuns who work in the facility exhibit the effects of symbolic violence. What's more, as upholders of the masculine social order, they reign over an institution whose residents regularly employ symbolic force to gain the upper hand over one another.

One can consider Mariotte's living situation a community only in that the residents of the home share a living space, the experience of old age, and the feeling of abandonment. Beyond that, they seem to be unified solely in their desire to humiliate their companions. Mariotte, for instance, approaches one of her fellow residents each morning, asking to borrow a pair of reading glasses, "deux misérables verres de nul usage au monde pour personne—sauf moi" (PP 24). [two miserable glasses of no use to anyone—except me.] Rather than simply give Mariotte the glasses, each morning the woman forces Mariotte to agree to certain conditions, such as massaging her legs or sacrificing her weekly dessert for a few hours of reading (PP 24–25). Another woman regularly dumps a glass of water on Mariotte in the middle of the night, an action that brings the narrator to tears (PP 13). It is not clear to the reader to what extent Mariotte participates in the trickeries of the home, but her notebooks indicate that she dehumanizes other residents through the symbolic violence of language. She refers to some of her companions only by their room numbers: "Le Huit du palier" (PP 34) [The Eight of the landing], "Le Dix-sept" (PP 182) [The Seventeen], or worse, gives them cruel nicknames, such as "La Pissette" (11) [The Pisser].

After having spent two years in the nursing home, Mariotte admits that she no longer believes in a reality that exists outside of its walls (PP 19). Instead, her "faith" is now tied solely to the suffering that she undergoes and witnesses on a daily basis. In one of her notebooks, Mariotte lists her beliefs in a passage reminiscent of Catholic creeds recited at mass and in saying the rosary. She reveals that she believes in the humid stone walls whose condensation could be the tears of the residents; she believes in the dead blue eyes of Sister Marie des Anges; and she believes in Madame Cormier, who is sure to die in the coming weeks: "Je crois en vous comme en tout ce qui se passe dans le Trou: sonorités et odeurs, délires et rêves, comédies cruelles et inlassables que nous nous donnons les unes les autres, faute de mieux car nous sommes juste assez proches pour nous haïr et non pas nous connaître, nous aimer, nous reconnaître" (PP 20–21). [I believe in you as in everything that happens in the Hole: sounds and odors, deliriums and dreams, cruel and tireless comedies that we give to one another, for lack of anything better, for we're just close enough to hate one another and not to know one another, to love one another, to recognize one another.] Mariotte's creed is indeed a desperate and mocking one. Given her experience in the nursing home, or the "Hole," as she prefers to call it, Mariotte has an understandable need to find reprieve in imagined returns to her childhood, even though they prove to be upsetting and mostly unfulfilling.

Mariotte's escape to her past resuscitates figures far removed from her by time and geography. This mental space that Mildred Mortimer calls "the inner world of imagination, spirituality, and memory" (ix) can serve as an empowering space for a female protagonist, but this is not the case for Mariotte. She claims that her journeys to this inner world of imagination simply represent a more humane pain than that which she suffers in the nursing home (PP 44). Yet her notebooks are evidence that this space of imagination does prove to be a fruitful space of creation in which Mariotte ponders the course her life has taken. When she permits herself to make her imagined returns to Martinique, Mariotte quickly finds her maternal grandmother, who reminds her of past humiliations and transgressions through her harsh criticisms. Yet her grandmother is not the one she seeks. In mentally returning to her childhood, she grovels for her own mother's forgiveness, hoping to alleviate the guilt she feels for not having died in the volcanic eruption that killed her family. Although these returns to her childhood never provide Mariotte and her dead mother with the kind of intense, one-on-one meeting that she has with her grandmother's specter, Mariotte's inner space allows her to recall the days leading up to her grandmother's death, when the whole family prepared for her passing. In her vision, Mariotte is thrilled to catch a glimpse of her mother's face, as she and Aunt Cydalise prepare their mother's final meal (PP 104). She also recalls visiting the prison with her mother to bring a serving of that last meal to Raymoninque, the prisoner who she suspects is her father. Knowing that she and most of her family members would go hungry that day, Mariotte recalls the angst that she felt when surrendering the precious food to the man who had never claimed her as his own: "J'ai posé la main gauche sous l'écuelle et j'ai fait une révérence-esclave à Raymoninque, afin qu'il n'y ait aucun doute, en ses âme et conscience, . . . que la nourriture lui était offerte des deux mains" (PP 133). [I placed my left hand under the dish and I bowed like a slave to Raymoninque, so that there be no doubt, in his soul and conscience, . . . that the food was offered to him with both hands.] Though Mariotte does succeed in "seeing" her mother once again, her animated visions of childhood are, for the most part, reminders of the hardships she experienced in Martinique. Her descriptions of her youth suggest that prolonged periods of hunger were not out of the ordinary, and she remembers that it is with great difficulty that she bowed "like a slave" as she sacrificed much-needed food to her mother's companion.

Mariotte's reflections illustrate that the bookends of her life—her childhood and her final years in the nursing home—are spent in settings wherein men and women respect and reinforce the masculine social order. At the end of her life, she finds herself in a hostile environment populated overwhelmingly by women, yet she still prostrates herself to one of the few men in the home when begging him for a glass of wine. Once again, a man holds a privileged and revered place amongst the many women who surround him. In refusing her a glass of wine, he uses sexually explicit language to suggest that her bad humor may be due to lack of sexual activity in recent months. Mariotte realizes that his offensive language deserves "une violence au moins égale à celle qu'il me faisait; mais je n'y parvenais pas, me sentant comme affaiblie, éblouie de honte" (PP 38). [a violence at least as equal to that which he exerted upon me; but I couldn't do it, feeling weakened, overwhelmed with shame.] In this instance, Mariotte identifies his language as "violent," evidence that she is aware of the symbolic force that he has just exerted upon her. Even though she is conscious of the dynamic that exists between them, she finds that she is unable to answer his symbolic violence with symbolic violence of her own. Instead, when he and other residents wield harsh language against her, she resorts to what Bourdieu calls "soft violence"— the use of magic, lies, or passivity to combat symbolic violence (PP 32).

The thoughts inscribed in the seven notebooks also represent a form of soft violence in which Mariotte privately acts out against the community. Her life story contains many lacunas, leaving the reader to wonder about the narrator's travels, love life, and family. Yet in spite of the incomplete nature of her journals, Mariotte consistently depicts the thread of oppression that unifies the episodes of her life. Both her present and past experiences demonstrate systems of symbolic violence in which she sometimes perpetuates her own oppression. Even though she criticizes the masculine social orders of her youth and her old age, her written protests prove to be rather soft ones.

THE AFTERLIFE: A SPACE OF HER OWN

There are many ways in which Ying Chen's *L'Ingratitude* sets itself apart from the other novels treated in this study, including the daughter's bitterness towards the mother and the mother's relative "voicelessness" as her daughter explains the process of her own suicide. Similar to the nursing home where Mariotte spends her days, the seemingly "placeless" zone in which Yan-Zi exists has few geographic references to help the reader situate the characters and better imagine her surroundings. Her anonymous city and anonymous home represent another heterotopic space in which a character's repression propels her to seek escape. Contrary to Mariotte's quest to see her deceased mother, Yan-Zi seeks to flee maternal influence.

In *L'Ingratitude*, the maternal voice is transmitted by the voice of her daughter, who committed suicide to escape from her domineering mother. This voice differs greatly from those in *Le bonheur a la queue glissante*, which strives to give the voiceless mother a voice. In this case, Yan-Zi seeks to condemn her mother and the way in which she chose to raise her daughter by revealing only the most unpleasant aspects of the mother's controlling personality. For example, in the following passage, the reader is aware of the guilt the mother imposes on her daughter as she grows up: "Or, maman disait toujours qu'il lui était mille fois plus pénible de me voir grandir que de me mettre au monde. Car, en grandissant, je lui ressemblais de moins en moins" (IG 20). [Yet, Mom always said that it was a thousand times more painful to see me grow up than to bring me to the world. For, in growing up, I resembled her less and less.] Towards the end of the novel, as the mother spends final moments with her daughter's ashes, she declares: "Je te préfère ainsi, commence-t-elle tout bas. Oui, je te préfère en poudre. Tu es très douce comme ça, très mignonne, sans épingles ni cornes" (IG 111). ["I prefer you like this," she quietly begins. "Yes, I prefer you in powder. You are very sweet like that, very cute, without pins and horns."] Yan-Zi paints a harsh and bitter mother bent on controlling even the minutest details of her adult daughter's life. She employs symbolic violence to harm her daughter, even in death. This verbal violence is much subtler than physical violence, and in this case, is invisible to outsiders, since nobody witnesses the post-funeral mother-daughter encounter. Verbal violence thus allows the mother to maintain the appearance of the suffering mother without revealing her excessively harsh treatment of Yan-Zi.

Prior to her daughter's suicide, the mother manages every aspect of the familial space, the family home. Her daughter and husband are expected to respect her authority. When the mother decides that Yan-Zi is to give up her room for a sickly uncle, she effectively kicks her daughter out of the house, announcing: "Ses ailes ont durci, elle va s'envoler maintenant" (IG 107). [Her wings have hardened, she will fly away now.] The narrator returns to her room one last time to pack her suitcase, remarking that she has no place of her own: "Je contemplai cette pièce où j'avais longtemps vécu. Comme si elle se trouvait au milieu d'un désert de sable traversé par le vent, les traces de ma vie y seraient vite effacées" (IG 108). [I contemplated this room where I had lived a long time. As if it were located in the middle of a sandy desert traversed by the wind, the traces of my life would quickly be erased.] Yan-Zi is attached to her bedroom, but she realizes that this family home is now a place that negates her presence. She believes that she will soon be forgotten and that "her" bedroom is in reality a blank canvas waiting to be occupied by its next inhabitant. Unlike Dounia, Yan-Zi's mother fosters an unwelcoming, hostile environment as a way to demonstrate her power over her daughter.

The urban setting, although indistinguishable from descriptions of other cities, is also linked to Yan-Zi and her relationship with her mother. Having grown up in this city, feeling stifled by her mother's control over her, the narrator associates images of the city with the negative feelings she harbors towards her mother: "Les taxis y passaient fréquemment, dépassant les bicyclettes avec fierté et ne pouvant s'empêcher de klaxonner de triomphe. Ces bruits aigus et secs rappelaient la voix de maman" (IG 20). [Taxis passed by frequently, passing bicycles with pride and not able to prevent themselves from honking in triumph. These shrill and dry sounds brought back Mom's voice.] The city may resemble other cities, but for the spectral narrator, it is a suffocating space that reminds her of the mother she abhors.

Before her death, she often frequents le Restaurant Bonheur [Happiness Restaurant] to escape the maternal influence and contemplate her impending suicide. The restaurant represents neither happiness nor distraction for Yan-Zi, and she even announces to the owner: "Je viens ici . . . parce que je ne sais pas où aller" (IG 19). [I come here . . . because I don't know where to go.] She spends her time in the restaurant contemplating her mother and begins her suicide note: "J'y dessinai le mot Maman avec application. . . . Le mot s'était trempé de crépuscules rougeâtres qui provoquaient mon écœurement" (IG 19). [I drew the word Mom with diligence. . . . The word was drenched in red crepuscules that provoked my disgust.] While writing offers Mariotte the opportunity to temporarily forget the present, Yan-Zi is unable to find any refuge in the act. Rather than serving as a liberating force, her creative inner space is tainted by her omnipresent mother.

Even at the Restaurant Bonheur, a place that her mother may never have visited, Yan-Zi allows herself to be overcome by the pressure she believes her mother exerts on her. As Yan-Zi reveals, the restaurant never really allows her to evade reality: "J'avais l'impression d'avoir passé ma vie à boire du thé dans ce restaurant, à attendre" (IG 72–73). [I had the impression that I had spent my life drinking tea in the restaurant, waiting.] Her visits to the restaurant quickly become part of the monotony of her life, along with days at the office and dreaded family meals.

In L'Ingratitude, space is important in that it illustrates the tension between the mother's authoritarian ways and her daughter's appetite for freedom. Both in life and death, the mother-daughter culture clash is Yan-Zi's principal focus and, one could even say, her obsession. The maternal voice and nameless mother are both overshadowed by the narrator who looks back on her life after her shameful suicide. The city's busy streets and park do not allow her to escape from her mother. It would seem that the mother's influence is so strong that no earthly place could provide refuge for Yan-Zi.

A woman's path can lead her through a variety of spaces, some which eventually become *places*, charged with sentiment. These spaces can be rural, urban, internal, oppressive, or freeing. As we have seen in this study, even in restrictive situations, women create. Feelings of loneliness and detachment can give way to expression. Reine Sans Nom and Télumée draw strength from the sense of stability they find in their garden. After years of solitude, Eliette transforms a space of solitude into a home for her adopted daughter. In a confined, unhappy nursing home, Mariotte escapes to her past through her imagination and journals about her mental travels. Dounia, too, taps into a creative mental space to contemplate the upheavals that have colored family life. Yan-Zi's story is perhaps the most tragic due to her suicide, but the spectral narrator nonetheless succeeds in telling her story on her terms. So, even death can inspire creation. As they move through different spaces, both physical and mental, each of these characters decides that she has something to share. And in confusing, dynamic, transcultural contexts, they create.

NOTES

1. See chapter 2.

2. I borrow geographer Yi-Fu Tuan's use of the terms *space* and *place*. Tuan explains that the notion of space is more abstract than that of place, as it is linked to the ideas of openness and freedom (6, 54). Place, on the other hand, incites feelings of familiarity and security and can be experienced in a town or city one knows well, in one's own home, or even with a loved one whose presence evokes a sense of comfort (Tuan 3, 29). The two are linked, as "space is transformed into place as it acquires definition and meaning" (Tuan 136).

3. One can surely place *Cahier d'un retour au pays natal* in the Francophone corpus due to its form, rhythm, and treatment of language. This text is closer to postcolonial than colonial tradition because of these elements and the subject matter of the poem.

4. See chapter 1 for a thorough explanation of Glissant's cultural theory.

5. Numerous critics have criticized Bhabba's theory on the Third Space, including Doneday, Fisher, Parry, and Dirlik, citing his lack of regard for gender, historical specificity, and his unorthodox reading of Fanon. For further discussion of Bhabha's Third Space, see chapter 1.

6. In this context, the patriarchy refers to two distinct groups: the men of her family and community, such as fathers, husbands, brothers, and neighbors, as well as the foreign colonizer whose influence is evident in both subtle and obvious ways.

7. The original inhabitants of the French Caribbean islands were the Arawak and Carib tribes, but they have been all but wiped out by European presence.

8. My emphasis.

9. The term *literature of place* is used in discussions of nature writing. It refers to the strong pull a particular region, landscape, or even small plot of land has on a person, calling him or her to write about the spot.

10. When using the term *Black Atlantic*, Nixon refers to writers such as Derek Walcott, Aimé Césaire, Wilson Harris, Patrick Chamoiseau, and Michelle Cliff.

11. Algeria was held by France from 1830–1962, an exceptionally long occupation by a foreign power. Marie Cardinal, a French author raised in Algeria, recounts her first post-independence visit to Algeria in *Au pays de mes racines*. In this work, she reveals the pull she feels to her Algerian homeland and the traumatic separation from the familiar surroundings she experienced upon her forced departure.

12. For more on religion in *Pluie et vent*, see "Espace féminin et image divine: vers une définition de la religion dans *Pluie et vent sur Télumée Miracle* de Simone Schwarz-Bart" by Maria Anagnostopoulou-Hieschler.

13. Heliconia is a tropical plant related to bananas and ginger, often with colorful leaves.

14. Toussine is given the name *Reine Sans Nom* after the birth of her daughter Victoire, so until that point in the novel she is referred to as *Toussine*.

15. An identitary space is one in which a person comes to understand him- or herself far from the reaches of a society that could hinder or taint that process.

16. One can hardly discuss gardens in literature without thinking of Colette's *Sido*. The garden serves as an escape from chores and family drama for this mother figure: "Elle atteignait, loyale, la fin de la tâche. Alors elle franchissait les deux marches de notre seuil, entrait dans le jardin. Sur-le-champ tombaient son excitation morose et sa rancune. Toute présence végétale agissait sur elle comme un antidote, et elle avait une manière étrange de relever les roses par le menton pour les regarder en plein visage" (Colette, *Sido* 10). [Loyal, she reached the end of her task. Then she crossed the two steps of our threshold, entering the garden. Right away, her morose agitation and her bitterness fell away. All vegetal presence acted on her like an antidote, and she had a strange way of lifting roses by their chin to look at them right in the face.] The garden serves as a healing space of freedom for Sido, yet she is free from the history of slavery and oppression found in literary gardens in literature of the French Caribbean.

17. Jumping between narrators incites a sense of imbalance on the part of the reader and a holistic picture of the community of Savane Mulet, since different points of view are expressed.

18. The use of the term *mauvaiseté*, rare in modern French, is important in that it indicates a belief in the occult, astrology, and other practices not explained by science and often shunned by mainstream societies.

19. I choose the term "childless mother" to describe Eliette because although she has never mothered a child, she *perceives* herself as a mother throughout her adult life. At different times she either waits for or searches out a child to mother, as she sees this as the principal role she is to fulfill in her life (EM 8–9, 20, 64).

20. The most recent hurricane referred to in *L'espérance-macadam* is Hurricane Hugo, one of the most destructive hurricanes in history, which struck Guadeloupe in 1989.

21. In an interview with Nadege Veldwachter, Pineau reveals her implicit intention to associate human behavior and nature: "I had a structure to follow since I had a theme: incest. I wanted to bring to life the forces of nature, their violence, and the violence of human beings. I wanted to evoke the whirling winds of the cyclones through a circular construction that grows denser and denser until you see the father commit this act of violence" (paragraph 6).

22. Food preparation, much like storytelling, is a means of preserving and transmitting culture. See "Reconstruire dans l'exil: la nourriture créatrice chez Gisèle Pineau" by Valérie Loichot and "Culinary diasporas: identity and the language of food in Gisèle Pineau's *Un papillon dans la cité* and *L'Exil selon Julia*" by Brinda J. Mehta. Loichot and Mehta both argue that when in exile, food is used not only to transmit culture but also to recreate the homeland.

23. Mariotte refers to the leaf she pulls from an envelope as a "feuille de siguine" (PP 45) [philodendron leaf]. Saint-John Perse's poem *Pour fêter une enfance* [*In Celebration of a Childhood*] contains an intertext that creates an intriguing link between the two works: "Que ta mere était belle, était pâle / lorsque si grande et lasse, à se pencher, / elle assurait ton lourd chapeau de paille ou de / soleil, coiffé d'une double feuille de siguine, / et que, perçant un rêve aux ombres dévoué, / l'éclat des mousselines / inondait ton sommeil!" [Oh how your mother was pretty, was pale / when so tall and limp, leaning down, / she took care of your heavy straw made of straw or of / sun, coiffed with a double philodendron leaf, / and that, piercing a devoted shadow dream, / the burst of chiffon / flooded your sleep!] In the context of the poem, like that of the novel, the leaf exists in a comforting, dream-like state.

24. In a talk titled *Des espaces autres* (1967), Michel Foucault labels retirement homes as heterotopias, or spaces of otherness. Prisons, cemeteries, gardens, and psychiatric hospitals are amongst the other heterotopias he includes in his analysis (1576).

4

DEATH

An Emotional Exile

After the unexpected death of his daughter Léopoldine, Victor Hugo wrote poems evoking images from her childhood and his despair following her death, many of them published in *Les Contemplations*. In the preface, Hugo explains that the reader should read the collection as the book of a dead man (25), thus establishing death as the framework of *Les Contemplations*. His sadness is manifest in many of the poems. *Oh! Je fus comme fou dans le premier moment* . . . explains the disbelief the father felt upon learning his child had died. *A Villequier* reveals that although grief has taken a toll on the poet, he maintains his faith in a higher power. Other poems capture tender memories from Léopoldine's childhood. *Elle avait pris ce pli* . . . recounts sweet morning moments shared between father and daughter, followed by a sad acknowledgment: "Et c'était un esprit avant d'être une femme" (Hugo 200). [And she was a spirit before becoming a woman.]

Demain, dès l'aube, perhaps Hugo's best-known poem, sets itself apart from the other poems in *Les Contemplations*. In this poem, he directly addresses his deceased daughter:

> Demain, dès l'aube, à l'heure où blanchit la campagne,
> Je partirai. Vois-tu, je sais que tu m'attends.
> J'irai par la forêt, j'irai par la montagne,
> Je ne puis demeurer loin de toi plus longtemps (Hugo 210)

[Tomorrow, at dawn, at the hour when the countryside brightens
I'll leave. You see, I know that you await me.
I'll go by forest, I'll go by mountain,
I cannot keep far from you any longer]

Through poetry, Hugo strives to maintain a relationship with his daughter, telling her that nothing can keep them apart. While Hugo often uses poetry as a vehicle to express grief or to celebrate his daughter's short life, *Demain dès l'aube* serves a different function. This poem attests to the father-daughter bond that Hugo nurtures even after Léopoldine's passing. The poet-father promises to traverse a great distance to be by her side, acknowledging the impatience that both feel to be with the other once again. So in addition to providing a space for expression of memories and emotional pain, literature can also serve as a forum for the living to cultivate their relationships with deceased loved ones.

Having lost a number of young family members, Hugo had given extensive consideration to the legacies of the deceased: "La beauté de la mort, c'est la présence. Présence inexprimable des âmes aimées, souriant à nos yeux en larmes. L'être pleuré est disparu, non parti. Nous n'apercevons plus son doux visage ; nous nous sentons sous ses ailes. Les morts sont les invisibles, mais ils ne sont pas les absents . . ." (qtd. Cheng 85). [The beauty of death is presence. Inexpressible presence of beloved souls, smiling at our teary eyes. The mourned being is deceased, not gone. We no longer see his sweet face; we feel that we are under his wings. The dead are the invisible ones, but they are not the absent ones.] Hugo perceives the deceased as an overarching, protective presence that evades comprehension.

Some contemporary Francophone authors also use literature as a space of exchange between the living and the dead. Whereas Hugo's poems exude tenderness and regret, the novels treated in this chapter deal with mysterious or shameful deaths that leave confused or angry survivors. Thus, the "inexpressible presence" of the dead is laden with angst, and death becomes a form of exile for both the deceased and their loved ones. This chapter examines the imaginary space of cultural exchange created upon the death of a mother or child in three novels: *La Femme sans sépulture* by Assia Djebar, *Des rêves et des assassins* by Malika Mokeddem, and *L'Ingratitude* by Ying Chen.

PHANTOMS, SPIRITS, SPECTERS, AND GHOSTS: "LIVING" AFTER DEATH

Writer François Cheng believes that contemplation of death gives sense and meaning to life. His *Cinq méditations sur la mort: autrement dit sur la vie* [*Five Meditations on Death: Otherwise Stated on Life*] insist on the richness life holds if one is conscious of his or her inevitable death. "Nous ne pouvons penser la vie sans penser la mort, pas plus que nous ne pouvons penser la mort sans penser la vie" (Cheng 42). [We cannot think about life without thinking about death any more than we can think about death without thinking about life.] Life and death are enmeshed, and people are ever aware of the relationship each has to the other. Cheng goes so far as to declare death the fruit of our being (41). In that vein, it is natural that death and its reverberations would inform family dynamics.

Upon losing a family member or close friend, a period of suffering often ensues in which one adjusts to the absence of that person. The trauma of loss can have a performative component in society and within families themselves. The terms *mourning* and *bereavement* are useful in discussion of literary depiction of death and grieving. *The Concise Oxford Dictionary* defines the word *bereavement* as "the fact or state of being deprived of anything, especially by death" and *mourning* as "the expression of deep sorrow, especially for a dead person, by the wearing of solemn dress" (*COD*). The two terms surely go hand-in-hand, but while *bereavement* can be a wholly private experience, *mourning* possesses a community-oriented dimension involving a public display of anguish.[1]

In her book *The Mourner's Dance*, Katherine Ashenburg traces the development of various mourning practices from antiquity to modern times, comparing the ways different societies mourn. She explains, for example, that the grieving share sorrow in a number of settings. Jews perform Kaddish, a daily public prayer said in Aramaic for eleven months after the death of a family member (Ashenburg 209). In secular societies, bereavement support groups, oftentimes meeting weekly, give mourners the opportunity to talk about their departed loved one with others who have experienced a similar loss.

Ashenburg notes that in most societies, gender plays a role in mourning rituals. She cites a traditional Ghanan practice in which women enter a trance-like state so as to channel the spirit of the dead, as well as *sati*, the Indian practice of widows throwing themselves in the funeral pyres of their deceased husbands (Ashenburg 157–158). Although certain religious groups assign specific mourning "tasks" to men such as ministers, rabbis, and priests who perform funeral ceremonies, it is women who perform most mourning rituals, including preparation of the corpse and organization and distribution of personal affairs: "Women, for whatever reason or reasons, appear to have a penchant for mourning" (Ashenburg 158). Traditionally confined to the domestic sphere, mourning practices have more or less remained in the hands of women: "For most of the world's history, death, like the life of a woman, was intensely domestic. It still is in some parts of the world" (Ashenburg 159). Our discussion of the selected novels will show that in Francophone postcolonial societies, bereavement and mourning rest solidly in the feminine domain. We will see that mourning periods linger and conform to no strict guidelines. Even if an official mourning period has come to a close, it is an individual experience whose beginning and end cannot be determined by outside forces. In Djebar's *La Femme sans sépulture*, for instance, the adult daughters of the legendary Zoulikha struggle with their mother's death and heroic heritage that haunt them some twenty years after her disappearance. Their mourning does not follow a conventional trajectory since they have never been able to provide their mother with a proper burial. In Mokeddem's *Des rêves et des assassins*, Kenza experiences a delayed mourning process, never having known her mother. It is only as a young adult that she seeks to understand her plight and finally to mourn the loss of the mother she does not remember. The mourning period can also be tainted by bitter mother-daughter disagreements carried over from life, as evidenced in *L'Ingratitude* by Ying Chen.

Although mourning and bereavement are common, sometimes shared experiences, individuals live those experiences differently. In her book *Comment j'ai vidé la maison de mes parents*, Lydia Flem recounts her own process of bereavement and mourning after the death of her parents. She explains that mourning is ultimately a solitary experience: "L'expérience du deuil se vit dans la solitude. Il n'est pas seulement douleurs et chagrins. Agressivité, colère, rage sont aussi au rendez-vous" (Flem 149). [The experience of mourning can be seen in solitude. It is not limited to pain and grief. Aggressiveness, anger, rage are also there.] Her mourning period coincides with the process of emptying her parents' home and sorting through all sorts of keepsakes and personal effects.

Thus, this wrenching period also entails moments of discovery or rediscovery of family history and of herself: "Je voulais savoir. Non plus être le contenant passif d'une trop grande douleur mais assumer l'histoire qui avait précédé ma naissance, comprendre l'atmosphère dans laquelle j'étais née" (Flem 75). [I wanted to know. No longer be the passive container of an unmanageable pain but assume the history that had preceded my birth, understand the atmosphere in which I had been born.] Flem reveals previously unknown details about her parents' lives as European Jews in the twentieth century, and in their absence she finally begins to understand how their trials influenced family relations. The emptying of their house, an emotionally wrenching project, ends up facilitating healing and advancing the mourning process:

> Se réconcilier avec ses morts, atteindre la sérénité du souvenir exige le lent dépôt du temps. Les saisons doivent reparaître une à une et la vie, pas à pas, geste après geste, l'emporter sur la mort. Si l'on traverse la tempête des sentiments sans en exclure aucun, aussi vif ou vil qu'il paraisse, si l'on donne son consentement à ce qui surgit en nous, peut éclore une légèreté nouvelle, une renaissance après le déluge, un printemps de soi-même. (Flem 12)

> [Reconciling with the deceased, attaining the serenity of memory requires the plodding of time. The seasons need to reappear one by one, and life, step by step, gesture after gesture, prevails over death. If we endure the storm of feelings without excluding any of them, as sharp or vile as it may seem, if we consent to that which surges up in us, a new lightness can bloom, a renaissance after the flood, a spring of one's self.]

Flem's journey reiterates the interrelated nature of life and death that Cheng celebrates. In facing the death of her parents, she begins to understand the course their lives took. Subsequently, clarity about her role arises. She comes to realize that writing is her contribution to the *matrimoine*[2] passed on to her through generations of handmade objects, including her mother's array of dresses, grandmother's embroidered table linens, and clothes hangers with covers crocheted by her great-grandmother (Flem 100–101). Although she is not capable of the same kind of domestic creations accomplished by her foremothers, she preserves the *matrimoine* in telling her story of grief and her quest for healing.

What link does Flem's memoir of mourning have with the novels examined in this chapter? Does her mourning experience parallel those of other Francophone women? Although Flem does not write in a postcolonial context, her Jewish heritage indicates a family history of discrimination, war, and displacement, experiences common to families living in a postcolonial setting. Her memoir shows that the process of mourning is riddled with past misunderstandings and unrevealed secrets. Emptying her parents' house forces her to unravel some of the enigmas that have defined her existence. The personal renaissance Flem experiences does not put an end to her grief. The last sentence of her book declares: "Je n'ai pas envie de mettre un point final à ce livre" (Flem 152). [I don't want to bring an end to this book.] She ends her story with no punctuation, indication of her desire to allow her evolving mourning process to continue. While she may have reconciled with her deceased parents, she has not finished mourning their loss. *Comment j'ai vidé la maison de mes parents* attests to an ongoing influence of the dead on the living.

The works examined in this chapter also evidence multi-dimensioned mourning processes with no clear finishing point. Whereas Hugo maintains a connection with his daughter through memory and Flem discovers truth while sorting through family belongings, a number of postcolonial works count on supernatural intervention to illustrate the ongoing interactions between the living and the dead. Characters who are not "gone" but have simply assumed another form of existence prove to be of great interest in postcolonial literature, providing commentaries on some of the challenges faced by contemporary Francophone societies, such as the struggle between tradition and modernity and the place of women in the public sphere.

The function of spectral characters in a postcolonial context is often linked to traumatic events experienced during the lifetime of that person, of either a personal or political nature. The spirits of the deceased seem to have unfinished business that prevents them from leaving the human plane, thus maintaining an earthly presence after death. In her book *Histoires de fantômes*, Martine Delvaux elaborates on the importance of the dead in the lives of the living: "Le travail du deuil est un travail possible-impossible, une tâche accomplie dans la mesure où elle ne doit pas l'être. Ce serait là une exigence éthique: ne pas enterrer les morts, ne pas oublier les fantômes, et les laisser nous hanter" (20). [The work of mourning is a possible-impossible job, a task accomplished in the measure where it shouldn't be. Herein would lie an ethical requirement: not to bury the dead, not to forget phantoms, and to let them haunt us.] The dead therefore maintain a presence, and "seeing" a ghost is not necessary for the memory of that person to forever function as a ghostly presence. In *La Femme sans sépulture*, Zoulikha remains on Earth in hopes of providing guidance for her daughter. In *L'Ingratitude*, an angry daughter who committed suicide to escape from her mother deals with the same harsh sentiments in the afterlife. Keltoum, the mother figure in *Des rêves et des assassins*, is voiceless both in life and death. The mystery surrounding her mother haunts Kenza, and as a young adult she feels compelled to seek clues about the last years of her mother's life, finally resuscitating her mother's memory. We will see that the loss of life, whether it be one's own or that of a family member, incites confusion, plunging characters into an emotional exile characterized by separation from the self, family members, or both.[3] Yet literature allows for the dead to speak in subtle and overt ways through the sharing of stories by those left behind or the incorporation of spectral voices who tell their own stories.

SPECTRAL EXILE: *LA FEMME SANS SÉPULTURE*

The epigraph preceding *La Femme sans sépulture*, a quotation from Louis-René des Forêt's *Poèmes de Samuel Wood*, evokes otherworldly voices that are difficult to remember and discern:

> Il y a pourtant en elle une chose qui dure
> Même après que s'en est perdu le sens
> Son timbre vibre encore au loin comme un orage (11)

> [There is nonetheless in it a thing that lasts
> Even after having lost the meaning
> Its tone still vibrates from afar like a storm]

The novel that follows attempts to recount the life of a heroine from Algeria's war of liberation through a chorus of women's voices, including that of the deceased. In recording their stories, Djebar breathes life into Zoulikha's memory, assuring that hers is a voice that persists.

The novel's Prelude places it in a musical context, introducing the story as might an overture to an opera. Divided into four sections, it draws the reader's attention to several themes that will be presented in the novel. Interweaving her own story with the heroine's, the author-narrator explains that both women had lived in her hometown Césarée, although at different times. She recalls her 1982 film *La Zerda ou les chants d'oubli*, dedicated to both the heroine and the Hungarian musician Béla Bartók.[4] Music has, in effect, already allowed Djebar to "hear" Zoulikha: "Peut-être que, grâce à la musique de Bartok, je l'entends, moi, j'entends Zoulikha constante, présente" (FS 17). [Maybe, thanks to Bartok's music, *I* hear her, I hear Zoulikha constant, present.] The author-narrator perceives Zoulikha as living above the streets, patios, and terraces of the city (FS 17). Zoulikha's daughters Hania and Mina also appear in the Prelude, highlighting their mother's bravery and rebellion against the injustices of the European occupation of Algeria.

The Prelude to *La Femme sans sépulture* announces the essential role of women's voices in the novel—that of the deceased heroine, her daughters, her friends, and the author-narrator. Djebar places those voices in successive chapters, side by side, creating a sort of literary polyphony wherein each woman relates her memories and grief. Rather than blend to "sing" the story of the heroine, the women's voices remain polyphonic, appearing side by side to transmit varied impressions of the heroine while remaining separate from one another. These, along with the four phantasmal monologues[5] of the deceased Zoulikha, serve to create a portrait of the mythical *maquisarde*.[6]

Zoulikha's friends and family members portray different episodes of her life: Zohra Oudia testifies to the heroine's calm when she is being pursued by the French police (FS 82–86); Dame Lionne tells about the complicated resistance network she allowed Zoulikha to run out of her home (FS 150–164); Hania relates the ten years of happiness her mother knew with her third and final husband (FS 57); and towards the end of the novel, Mina, for the first time, speaks of the days she spent in a cave with her mother and the other members of the *maquis* shortly before her mother's disappearance (FS 211–215). Essential links between the past and present, these testimonials demonstrate many dimensions of Zoulikha's personality and serve to illustrate some of the ways in which women contributed to the liberation effort. Yet when we examine her death as a form of exile, the heroine's portrayal of *herself* is of great interest. How does the ghostly figure perceive her life and death? How do her life and afterlife relate? What messages do her monologues convey?

In the second chapter of this study, we examined how Zoulikha's absence continues to affect her daughters years after her disappearance. The heroine's spectral voice reveals that she, too, suffers so many years after her torture and death. Laroussi views the monologues as a refusal to be buried a second time (193), and O'Riley sees them as a way to reappropriate history (66). These observations are justified, as Zoulikha often references political topics such as the place of women in contemporary Algerian society (FS 223) and torture of prisoners (FS 217–221). Zoulikha also shares anecdotes from the happy times spent with Mina's father (FS 190–193), attesting to her desire to be remembered.

Yet both O'Riley and Laroussi neglect the underlying maternal concern that is a motivating force behind the spirit's monologues. The heroine explains that she began speaking to Mina shortly after her death: "C'est à partir de cette aube que, dorénavant, je te parle, ô Mina, ma petite. Toi que je cherche dehors, dont je tente de deviner la voix là-bas, la présence, les mouvements, le travail" (FS 222). [Ever since that dawn I have been speaking to you, oh Mina, my little one. You whom I seek outside, whose voice I try to discern there, the presence, the movements, the work] The spectral narrator implies that she is forever at her daughter's side, both absent and present (FS 71), watching, speaking, and that after twenty years her soliloquy is becoming "un chant presque glorieux" (FS 185). [an almost glorious song.] That song, one that serves as her chronicle of the war of liberation and her critique of contemporary society, is principally concerned for her daughter who lives in Algeria's post-liberation society. Zoulikha's monologues are therefore comprised of interwoven and overlapping familial and societal concerns. Yet the dialogue she seeks to undertake with her daughter is never realized.

Addressing Mina in each monologue, the heroine admits to monitoring the young woman and her friends: "Vous, à votre tour, et ensemble, vous marchez enfin 'nues'" (FS 189). [You, for your part, and together, you are finally walking around "nude."] Proud of her unveiled daughter, Zoulikha sees a bit of her own rebellious spirit in Mina. Her discourse emanates a sense of validation as she undoubtedly feels that her own defiant behavior in some way paved the way for her daughter. Zoulikha's "song" touches on political questions of importance in contemporary Algeria, that of the veil and of women in the public sphere, with the underlying intention of informing and supporting her daughter. Her interest in current events and politics stems from her inherent concern for her child, not necessarily from a desire to perpetuate her legendary status or to disseminate a feminist discourse. The spirit of Zoulikha has shifted its focus to her daughter. She is now "living" for her. Her afterlife devotion to her child does not negate the brave actions accomplished during her lifetime, nor does it diminish her fame. It does, however, hint at guilt experienced by the heroine—guilt for having left her children to join the *maquis*, guilt for having died and left them to fend for themselves in post-war Algeria.

Zoulikha's spectral voice explains that she remains on Earth due to fear, a fear once linked to the torture she underwent before her death, but that she has since transferred to her fragile daughter. She lingers because she worries about Mina's well-being: "Comment puis-je rejoindre le royaume des morts rassérénée si me hantent encore mon angoisse pour toi, ma curiosité frileuse, ma faim nullement rassasiée de ton destin, toi, tige de jasmin risquant de tomber avant d'exhaler son parfum tenace" (FS 224). [How can I calmly join the kingdom of the dead if I am still haunted by my agony for you, my jumpy curiosity, my unsatisfied hunger for your destiny, you, jasmine stem risking to fall before having exhaled her tenacious perfume.] The myth of Zoulikha continues to trouble her daughters, but Zoulikha, too, admits to being haunted by agony and curiosity linked to Mina's unsure destiny. As a mother, she worries that her youngest daughter is stifled by her mother's heroic legacy and terrible death and that Mina will never blossom due to the fear connected to that tragic legacy. Will her mother's violent and untimely death prevent Mina from living? Djebar provides no clear answer to this question, but at the end of the book, Mina does, for the first time, speak in detail about the final days she spent with her mother.

Zoulikha hovers on a border between the living and the dead, voicing concerns and reliving key moments of her life. The afterlife provides her with a space of contemplation and expression that would not be available to her in contemporary Algeria. Beyond the reach of authority, she is free to share history as she remembers it. Yet her freedom is not victorious, as she experiences constant solitude, difficulty in communication, and separation from her family and friends. Death has thrown her into exile. Throughout the novel, Zoulikha's disconnection from her children is evident, as her "song" has gone unacknowledged for decades. The specter also confirms feeling cut off from her body: "Mon corps fait-il la sieste? . . . Comme s'il n'y avait plus jamais, pour moi, de nuit: le temps, l'espace, les courbes autour de mon corps refusant de pourrir, ou de s'émietter, tout n'était que lumière blanche—" (FS 224–225). [Is my body napping? . . . It was if there would never again be, for me, night: time, space, curves around my body refusing to rot, or to break down, there was only white light.] Confusion and disappointment mingle as the specter adjusts to the afterlife—no time, no space, only light and an inert body that refuses to decompose. So she is not only separated from her family, but she also must navigate a sort of exile from her perception of herself.

Although Zoulikha insists she is present among her loved ones, her voice is indiscernible to them in her formless state. The creative space of exchange that death offers the heroine is therefore an unsatisfying one. She speaks, but someone must be able to hear and inscribe her "song." In this context, the role of the author-narrator is essential. Drawn to the heroine's story yet free from familial burdens, she chronicles Zoulikha's life in both film and literature. Much as Zoulikha's afterlife exile frees her from the constraints of life in post-liberation Algeria, Djebar's extended absence from home allows her to criticize Algerians for having chosen "amnesia" (FS 236) over remembering the service of Zoulikha and others like her.

Acting as a companion to the Prelude, the Epilogue once again connects author and heroine. Writing from both Paris (June 1981) and New York (September 2001), Djebar laments her delay in completing the novel (FS 239). During a brief visit home, she senses Zoulikha: "Auparavant, ayant déployé une parole publique, lyrique, il me semble qu'elle s'est, pour ainsi dire, envolée. . . . Or son chant demeure" (FS 236). [Before, having deployed a public, lyrical voice, it seems to me that she has, so to say, flown away. . . . Yet her song remains.] Connected by geography and by gender, Djebar brings Zoulikha's story out of the silence she encounters in Algeria. The women's voices she puts forth, hers included, represent an act of resistance against conditions in post-liberation Algeria. At the end of the Epilogue, though, she brings to light another motivation for this novel on loss, mourning, and remembrance: "Quand serai-je vraiment de retour pour gravir le chemin qui monte au sommet de Césarée? Là où, sous mille couches de ténèbres, dort désormais mon père, les yeux ouverts" (FS 243). [When will I actually be back to go up the path that leads to the summit of Césarée? Where, under a thousand layers of darkness, from now on my father sleeps, eyes open.] Djebar's exile prevents her from properly mourning her deceased father. The last lines of *La Femme sans sépulture* join the various feminine voices through the act of mourning. Like the women who "sing" Zoulikha's story, Djebar lives a *deuil impossible*, or impossible mourning. Due to their circumstances, each woman is unable to mourn according to the customs of her society. Consequently, Djebar's novel becomes a public space of mourning that demonstrates the universality of grief.

ESCAPE BECOMES EXILE

The heroine in *La Femme sans sépulture* died in middle age after having been married and divorced, borne three children, and fought in a war. Her life was eventful and her death honorable. In Ying Chen's novel *L'Ingratitude*, the spirit we encounter is newly deceased, and the days following her suicide are documented by the angry spirit as she experiences a bumpy transition to the afterlife.[7] Like Zoulikha, Yan-Zi's spirit observes her family, comments on their activities, and attempts to communicate with them. At the same time, she waits for the glorious moment when she will be welcomed into heaven, but that moment does not come. Contrary to Zoulikha's passionate monologues directed to her daughter, Yan-Zi's voice is one of frustration and anger with her controlling mother whose grips she attempted to escape in committing suicide. The conditions of Zoulikha and Yan-Zi's lives and deaths are vastly different, but comparison of their spectral discourses provides varying perspectives on grief, mourning, and death as a potential space of creation.

Silvie Bernier's article "Ying Chen: s'exiler de soi" discusses an exile from the self as a theme in Chen's novels. This exile involves a rejection of and separation from one's past, therefore immersing oneself in another existence, geographically and emotionally removed from one's former self. In *L'Ingratitude*, death simultaneously creates an exile from the self and from the mother, as the uncommonly close mother-daughter identification prevents the narrator from making a life for herself:

> —J'ai envie d'être moi, maman.
> —Tu ne peux pas être toi sans être ma fille.
> —Je suis d'abord moi.
> —Tu as vécu d'abord dans mon ventre. (116)

[—I want to be me, Mom.
—You can't be you without being my daughter.
—I'm first and foremost me.
—First you lived in my stomach.]

This sparse yet revelatory dialogue between mother and daughter illustrates a confining relationship where individuality and self-expression are not options. As long as she is on the Earth and living under her mother's roof, Yan-Zi has no identitary separation between her and her mother. For Yan-Zi's mother, the Confucian value of obedience to one's parents takes precedent over any personal quest. As Yan-Zi looks back on her life from the foggy space she now inhabits, she admits to having wondered if she could live without her mother and what would become of her if she wasn't her daughter anymore (IG 98). Yan-Zi was never allowed to distinguish herself from her mother due to the harsh rules imposed in the household. So, in attempting to cut herself off from her mother through suicide, she in fact imposed an exile from the only "self" she ever knew—that of her mother, who was involved in every aspect of Yan-Zi's life. In the time following her death, Yan-Zi's specter comments on their tense relationship and observes her mother, hoping to see signs of sorrow and defeat. This proves to be a most unsatisfying experience for the spirit, as the mother refuses to be destroyed by grief.

After her death, the ghost of Yan-Zi quickly realizes that she has not succeeded in separating herself from the mother she detests. Rather, she is condemned to observe funeral preparations, hear the hurtful comments people make about her family, and even attend her own funeral dinner (IG 62–66). This is not the afterlife she had anticipated, and as always, she finds herself drawn to her mother:

J'inspire et retiens mon souffle pour me donner du poids. Je plonge. Je veux m'approcher de maman. J'aimerais moi aussi mettre une main sur son épaule inaccessible. Mais la fumée me repousse constamment. Sur la frontière entre la vie et la mort, cette fumée se comporte en gardienne implacable. (IG 11)

[I inhale and hold my breath to give myself weight. I plunge. I want to get close to Mom. I, too, would like to place a hand on her inaccessible shoulder. But the smoke constantly pushes me back. On the border between life and death, this smoke acts as a tenacious guardian.]

The spectral narrator sees and hears the funerary rituals, even witnesses her mother's grief, yet cannot reach her through death's fog. Her mother's expression of emotion sparks concern in the spectral narrator, and in one of her few displays of compassion, she attempts to comfort her mother. The above passage reveals that in death, as in life, Yan-Zi remains silent in her mother's presence. She tries to approach her mother yet never tries to *speak* to her. Also maintaining the dominant role she has always played, the mother chastises her deceased daughter. Addressing the box of ashes, she goes on an accusatory, bitter rant: "Ton silence aujourd'hui est plus authentique que jamais . . . mais ton silence suffit pour me calmer maintenant, me sauver du désarroi dans lequel tu as voulu me pousser. Ton ultime insulte se défait avec ton corps" (IG 111). [Your silence today is more authentic than ever . . . but your silence suffices to calm me now, save me from the helplessness in which you wanted to push me. Your final insult is unraveling with your body.] Her mother goes on to shame her daughter for the disruption she has caused in the family, chide her for defying tradition, and justify her own behavior as an attempt to protect her daughter from the "scars of life" (IG 111–112). Yan-Zi ended her life, yet the mother-daughter dynamic remains constant. Even in the confusing, smoke-filled space of death, mother and daughter struggle with disappointment in the other.

Being "new" to the afterlife, Yan-Zi repeatedly expresses her annoyance at being excluded from earthly activities and, most of all, her inability to interact with her mother. In Djebar's *La Femme sans sépulture*, Zoulikha seems to accept her spectral state after twenty years of observing the world evolve in her absence. She does not expect the living to hear what she dubs her "song," one composed out of concern for her daughter's destiny. Rather, Zoulikha's spirit is resigned to the fact that she will maintain her spectral existence out of need to keep some form of contact with her daughter. As hovering spectral beings, Zoulikha and Yan-Zi both experience ineffective communication with loved ones left on Earth. The frustration they encounter is linked to their respective exilic experiences, as it reinforces the solitude imposed by death. For both spectral narrators, death seems to function more as a space of creation than a space of exchange. Alone in the afterlife, they observe, remember, and initiate contact with the living. The specters end up mourning the lives they lost or, in Yan-Zi's case, the life she never lived. Although the evasive contact they seek is unsatisfying, it fuels creation. Over the years,

Zoulikha composes and perfects her account of her life through remembrance and contemplation. Perhaps even more remarkably, Yan-Zi is actually able to exercise her voice for the first time. Even though she does not speak to her mother and expresses angst at their separation, she nevertheless finds the freedom to describe her life as she experienced it. The trauma of maternal separation is in itself a gift, as it frees the lonely spirit to create her own story, apart from tradition and expectations.

The beginning of this chapter established literature as a means for the living to maintain relationships with the dead, underlining the important social function of mourning. Similarly, literature also reflects a space where we can imagine how the deceased might cope with loss of human connection and face anger carried over from life. Yan-Zi has not yet adjusted to the exile she encounters in death, having died only recently. She continues to deal with the anger brought on by generational conflicts she and her mother never overcame. This transcultural space is therefore replete with negative feelings, as her resentment towards her mother festers. Her disquiet is also linked to the circumstances of her death. In the restrictive family environment dominated by her mother, the only thing that could possibly have been worse than Yan-Zi's blossoming sexuality was suicide. Yan-Zi's suicide was an effort to devastate her mother and quash family dynamics dictated by Confucian values, but her death does not create the maternal misery she had intended. Contrary to Zoulikha's heroic death, Yan-Zi's was a shameful one. Even though both women sought liberty—Zoulikha from French oppression and Yan-Zi from maternal oppression—Zoulikha is a source of pride for her survivors, and Yan-Zi is a source of disgrace. That shame explains Yan-Zi's need to recount the most painful, minute details of her suicide planning, such as her consideration of ways she might kill herself: "J'avais longuement réfléchi aux méthodes. J'avais d'abord songé à sauter par la fenêtre de chez nous. De cette façon, je pourrais enfin laisser entendre à maman que je n'étais pas heureuse à la maison" (IG 55). [I had thought long and hard about methods. I first thought about jumping from the window of our house. This way, I could finally make Mom understand that I wasn't happy at the house.] The flood of words and images that surge from the confused, angry spirit comprise what Lucie Lequin calls the "journal of a suicide" (210), revealing the tragic thought process leading Yan-Zi to take her life. Her raw emotions are a contrast to Zoulikha's refined tone, honed in the twenty years of her ghostly exile.

Throughout *L'Ingratitude*, Yan-Zi painfully unravels her distressing and negative feelings towards her mother, all while watching the mother carry on without her. This proves to be an unpleasant experience, as she discovers that her suicide did not cause as much maternal suffering as Yan-Zi had hoped: "Elle retient les sanglots et les larmes. Elle refuse les consolations. La mort de sa fille constitue pour elle plus un échec personnel qu'une perte sentimentale" (IG 110). [She is holding back sobs and tears. She is refusing to be consoled. For her, the death of her daughter constitutes a personal failure more than a sentimental loss.] Although Yan-Zi is upset by her mother's icy reaction to her death, she does have the satisfaction of "owning" her death. Cheng emphasizes that death reveals itself as "la dimension la plus intime, la plus secrète, la plus personnelle de notre existence" (21). [the most intimate, secret, the most personal dimension of our existence.] The narrator's mother managed many aspects of her life yet could not give or take this death. Consequently, Yan-Zi's suicide is the one part of her life over which her mother had no say and is therefore the ultimate rejection of maternal control.

Does Yan-Zi, like Zoulikha, commit to staying connected to the human plane in hopes of communicating with her mother or waiting to see her suffer? She seems to have less control over her soul's movement than does Zoulikha. Little by little, she loses her earthly connections, eventually admitting that she no longer knows left from right, up from down, and has completely lost any sense of direction (IG 130). Her soul seems to be dissolving, and Yan-Zi does not care to halt the process. At the end of the book, as her spirit finally disconnects from Earth, she gains a new perspective:

Et moi aussi, je flotte. Je vais très loin. Pour la première et la dernière fois, sans doute, j'écoute les murmures des Alpes, je touche la chaleur du Sahara, je bois les eaux amères du Pacifique. Tout paraît très beau quand il n'y a plus de choix à faire, quand on aime sans objet, quand Seigneur Nilou ne vient pas,[8] quand on n'a plus de destin. (IG 133)

[And *I* too float. I'm going far away. For the first and last time, without a doubt, I'm listening to the murmurs of the Alps, I touch the heat of the Sahara, I drink the bitter waters of the Pacific. Everything appears very beautiful when there are no more choices to make, when one loves indiscriminately, when Seigneur Nilou doesn't come, when one no longer has a destiny.]

Yan-Zi has lost all motivation, all contact with the Earth, and she claims that all the hate she once possessed was burned with her corpse (IG 130). In releasing disdain, Yan-Zi opens herself to beauty she was never capable of seeing when she was focused on resentment. Death seems to sharpen her awareness of fleeting earthly beauties. In pondering the interplay between life and death, Cheng explains that the ephemeral and unexpected nature of beauty sharpens our awareness of death (83). The opposite is true for Yan-Zi. Prior to her death, oppression and unhappiness had obscured the loveliness she finally experiences as she releases hate and loves indiscriminately. The overwhelming beauty of the Earth moves her when it is almost too late to appreciate it.

Does her final departure mark an end to her emotional exile? Does awareness of beauty soften her outlook? While the word forgiveness is never mentioned, the end of the book has a tone of resignation—the spirit no longer expresses her *ingratitude*. Rather, she seems to have accepted her self-inflicted death and mother's willingness to continue without her. Yan-Zi's "post-life" existence has thus far been trying, but when she finally lets go of the anger and bitterness directed towards her mother, her perspective changes. Life after death has not proven to be a paradise, but as she detaches herself from the human plane, she finally is able to experience, for the first and last time, the world outside the oppressive environment she has always known. In leaving the Earth, she is aware of mountains, deserts, and bodies of water. Yan-Zi's transcultural experience has thus far been represented by a painful mother-daughter generational clash. For her, death is exile, and the tensions that weighed on her before her suicide also occupy the vague, transcultural space of death. Yet, as Yan-Zi floats away, anger and tension dissipate. For the first time, the narrator slips into a neutral tone, and in the last moments before her soul disappears, she witnesses some of the Earth's natural splendor. Although Yan-Zi leaves her mother behind, the maternal image is a lasting one, as the last word of the book is "Maman!" (IG 133) [Mom!] As her soul fades away, her spirit ceases to exist, the exile comes to a close, and her last memory is of her mother.

A SURVIVOR'S EXILIC EXISTENCE

The spectral narrators in *L'Ingratitude* and *La Femme sans sépulture* attest to an *existence* after death, if not a *life* after death, through description of the spaces they haunt and the living family members they attempt to contact from the indistinct zones they inhabit after death. The spaces inhabited by Zoulikha and Yan-Zi embody not only their personal stories of suffering but also come to represent exile and how it can be experienced in a transcultural context. They are at times lonely, confused, angry, and frustrated because they are disconnected from the spaces they consider home and those they have left behind.

In *Des rêves et des assassins*, Malika Mokeddem tells the story of a young woman named Kenza who has lived a "motherless" existence with no memories and little information about her mother who had left Algeria to live in Montpellier, France: "Ma mère, elle, je ne l'ai jamais connue. Ma prime enfance est marquée par son absence autant que par les excès de mon père. Le manque et l'outrance. Deux énormités opposées et sans compensation"[9] (RA 10). [My mother, I never knew *her*. My childhood is marked by her absence as much as by the extremes of my father. Emptiness and excess. Two opposed enormities and without compensation.] Her father, whom she paints as a sexual monster, in no way attempts to fill the void left by the absent mother. Instead, he and his second wife create an atmosphere in which Kenza is not welcomed as a part of the family, isolated from her half-siblings, and sent away at each and every school vacation (RA 14). As soon as she is old enough, she goes to boarding school, and she never returns to the paternal home: "Dès que j'ai pu me débrouiller seule, c'est moi qui ai fui mon père, sa bestialité, ses criailleries de sa marmaille, sa femme-servante, l'ambiance de cet immeuble devenu un étouffoir" (RA 15). [As soon as I could get along on my own, I'm the one who fled my father, his brutality, his brood's whining, his servant-wife, the ambiance of this building that had become suffocating.] Removed from paternal control, Kenza continues to thrive academically but does not develop friendships with the other girls at school. The isolation she experienced in the family home has carried over to the boarding school.[10]

The bits and pieces of information Kenza has gleaned over the years, including rumors of her mother's attempt to "kidnap" her infant daughter during a visit to Oran (RA 17), do not suffice to paint a portrait of the mother. Her mother's absence and father's rancor have created a vacuum in Kenza's life—one that she carries into her adult years. She is never able to properly grieve for her mother, for she cannot even imagine what it might be like to have a maternal figure in her life. She lives in an emotional exile brought on by maternal absence and paternal disregard. Like Zoulikha's daughter Mina, Kenza moves through much of her life mechanically, refusing or unable to build lasting relationships. Yet after falling in and out of love for the first time, her need to know about her mother surfaces:

> Dire qu'avant de rencontrer l'amour, j'ai avancé tendue vers un seul but: un examen, un diplôme. Les uns après les autres, ceux-ci m'aidaient à occulter mes manques, mes complexités et la schizo-phrénie grandissante du pays. Dire que la découverte de l'amour m'a plongée dans l'urgence vitale d'y étancher mes soifs. (RA 72)

> [Let's say that before finding love, I moved directly toward a single goal: an exam, a diploma. One after the other, these helped me conceal my empty spaces, my complexities, and the country's growing schizo-phrenia. Let's say that the discovery of love plunged me into the vital urgency of quenching my thirsts.]

Having finally loved and been loved for the first time, Kenza knows she must seek information about Keltoum. Her need to understand her origins reminds us of Flem's mourning process and the desire she expresses to know her own family history. Kenza's decision to leave France in search of her mother's story marks the beginning of her mourning process, some twenty years after the mother's death. The need to discover her deceased mother also happens to coincide with her need to flee Algeria's oppres-sive, frightening political atmosphere dominated by the FIS.[11]

When she arrives in Montpellier, the city of her birth, she sets out to find a friend of her mother's who had contacted Kenza many years prior. That mission proves to be difficult, as Kenza's only clue is a name—Zana Baki—and she discovers that as in Algeria, North African women tend to remain hidden in the private domain.[12] Nonetheless, for the first time in her life, Kenza becomes aware of her mother's presence in the streets of Montpellier. She searches for Keltoum in each and every North African woman who crosses her path and tries to imagine the places her mother may have frequented. Until this moment, the place a mother might have held in Kenza's life has been a void, representative of the emotional exile in which she functioned for most of her life. She has neither a positive nor negative maternal image due to the fact that no maternal figure has ever been in her life. Yet in Montpellier she begins to imagine the person her mother may have been: "Pour l'heure, la recherche de Zana Baki n'est qu'un leurre. C'est qu'en chacune d'elles, j'ai le sentiment étrange de croiser un spectre de ma mère. Comme si elle était toujours là, ma mère, fantôme errant, en plusieurs exemplaires" (RA 84). [For the moment, the search for Zana Baki is nothing but an illusion. In each of them, I have the strange feeling of seeing a specter of my mother. As if she were still there, my mother, wandering phantom, in multiple copies.] Her departure from Algeria allows the ghost of her mother to finally "come alive." In the country where Keltoum spent her last years, her daughter has the freedom to seek out those who may have known her and to "construct" a maternal vision. When Kenza does come into contact with two women who knew her mother, the stories they tell about Keltoum plant bitter-sweet images in the daughter's mind: after having lost her daughter, Keltoum's guilt and loneliness led her to attempt suicide (RA 147–148); mother and daughter share a fascination with the sea (RA 148); Keltoum always returned from the market with a bouquet of flowers; an illegal abortion took her life (RA 141). These personal details make the mother real. Kenza now possesses concrete images of her mother, and for the first time she is able to create and possess feelings of love and longing for her. Keltoum's story, heartbreaking for her daughter to hear, nonetheless gives Kenza a sense of validation and allows her to create a portrait of her mother—a young, troubled woman whose status as woman and immigrant caused much suffering.

Valérie Orlando has remarked that in exile, Algerian writers like Mokeddem carve a space that is simultaneously feminine, feminist, and North African ("Ecriture d'un autre lieu" 103). From that space, authors can express themselves freely. Similarly, for Chen's and Djebar's narrators, the spectral space is an enunciatory space free from the confines imposed by society before death. In *La Femme sans sépulture*, Zoulikha openly critiques contemporary Algerian society and strives to reconstruct a history that accurately portrays the important roles women played in Algeria's war of liberation, two things she never could do had she survived the war. Yan-Zi, as she floats above the Earth, uses her words to paint the repressive symbolic violence that traps each generation of women in her family. That subtle yet imposing violence impeded her in life and led her to commit suicide. Yet, as a specter, Yan-Zi is finally allowed to convey and comment on that inhibitive societal structure.

Kenza, too, learns to create a space of expression from her emotional exile. When, at the age of seventeen, one of her younger half-brothers reaches out to her, Kenza begins to realize just how isolated she is. After an uncomfortable, mostly silent visit, he leaves her with these words: "Ecris-moi au lycée, si tu as besoin de moi. C'est peut-être plus facile d'écrire que de parler" (RA 26). [Write to me at school, if you need me. Maybe it's easier to write than talk.] Caught off guard by his effort to connect with her, she feels both disturbed and disoriented following his visit (RA 27). Yet she contacts him, and the siblings tentatively begin to know one another during silent walks around Oran and then through the exchange of books. Finally, they begin to speak to one another: "Comme si tous les kilomètres parcourus, toutes les lassitudes atteintes, toutes les pages lues avaient été autant de chemins vers un but insoupçonné, la véritable rencontre. La communion des idées" (RA 30). [As if all the kilometers walked, all the weariness suffered, all the pages read had been paths toward an unsuspected goal, the true meeting. The communion of ideas.] Becoming acquainted with her brother is not only Kenza's first foray into family life but also the first time she feels close to another human being. Their effort of getting to know the other is at first a silent, awkward experiment between what the narrator labels "two solitudes" (RA 28). Both through and in their respective emotional exiles, Kenza and her half-brother do the painstaking work that eventually leads them to speak and share ideas with one another.

While the siblings build and maintain a trusting relationship that lasts into adulthood, Kenza has by no means carved a space of enunciation where she can express herself in the uninhibited manner of the spirits in *L'Ingratitude* and *La Femme sans sépulture*. The work begins with her half-brother and accelerates once she has left Algeria in search of the truth surrounding her deceased mother. The knowledge Kenza garners in Montpellier allows her mourning process to move forward, and as we have repeatedly observed, mourning the loss of a loved one is a consuming process.[13] The anxiety and sadness she experiences surface in a dream:

Je suis un fantôme. J'erre dans les ruines d'Oran. Sous un ciel de
sang. . . . Vrille une douleur dans ma tête et mon ventre. J'essaie de me
raisonner: un spectre ne peut pas souffrir. Il n'a ni tête ni ventre.
Qu'est-ce qui m'arrive? Quelque chose s'est encore détraqué en moi et
pourtant je suis morte. (RA 145)

[I am a phantom. I wander in the ruins of Oran. Under a sky of
blood. . . . A pain bores into my head and stomach. I try to reason with
myself: a specter cannot suffer. It has neither head nor stomach. What
is happening to me? Something has again become unhinged in me and
yet I am dead.]

In her disturbing dream, she encounters her own ghostly self, an acknowledgment of the spectral existence she leads as she uncovers details of her
mother's life. In *Specters of Marx*, Derrida avers the importance of talk-
ing with ghosts: "Not how to make conversation with the ghost but how
to talk with him, with her, how to let them speak or how to give them
back speech, even if it is in oneself, in the other, in the other in oneself:
they are always there, specters, even if they do not exist, even if they are
no longer, even if they are not yet" (14). Removed from the strains of life
in Algeria, Kenza awakens her own troubled spirit and finds the courage
to give back speech to the ghost of self that moves about in her sleep.

Montpellier is a transformational place for Kenza, and once she has
discovered the truth about her mother's life, she finds herself on a threshold between her former existence and one that will undoubtedly define
the next years of her life. As Kenza begins to emerge from her long-term
emotional exile, she is struck by fears and emotions she previously had
not had to face, not having known that her mother's final years had been
solitary and painful. Unwilling to return to the uncertain and restrictive
life Oran offers her, she uses Montpellier as a springboard for further
travels, announcing to a new friend: "Il me prend des envies de voyage.
Des envies d'aller vers des pays où je n'ai aucune racine" (RA 155). [I
want to travel. Want to go to countries where I have no roots.] It seems
that for a time, she will maintain her liminal existence as she visits places
with no family links.

Kenza, Zoulikha, and Yan-Zi seek to traverse the chasms between the
living and the dead, bypassing "official" histories put forth by their respective patriarchal societies. Although lonely, their spectral existences
allow them to form spaces of expression in which they weave their own

stories—stories that touch on tragedy and reveal injustice. Yet the act of telling their heavy stories is hopeful. Zoulikha imagines freedom for her daughter, Yan-Zi finally acknowledges beauty, and Kenza envisions a period of travel, far from the constraints of painful memories. They leave no doubt that death inflicts trauma, yet each of the three characters also uncovers the creative possibilities of bereavement and solitude as they explore the solitary space brought on by separation and sadness.

NOTES

1. The French language does not distinguish between the ideas of mourning and bereavement. The term *deuil* is used to express both notions: *faire le deuil*—to mourn, *porter le deuil*—to wear mourning clothes.

2. *matrimoine*—In opposition to the term *patrimoine*, or patrimony, Flem employs the term *matrimoine* to indicate that which is passed down through mothers. I include this term in the French, as there is no equivalent in English. The direct translation *matrimony* refers to the institution of marriage rather than the act of communicating tradition and culture.

3. I borrow the idea of exile from the self from Silvie Bernier's article "Ying Chen: s'exiler de soi," in which she analyzes the narrators in four of Chen's novels as characters whose empty existences equate to an exile from the self and one's own life and personal history. Bernier considers these characters as reflections of Chen's own choice to write in French rather than in Mandarin Chinese, representing her own exile from the self, that is to say, her separation from her culture and her past.

4. Béla Bartók, a twentieth century Hungarian composer, was a founder of comparative musicology. He studied and collected folk music from different parts of the world, seeing relevance in the influence of place and tradition on music.

5. See discussion of the monologues in chapter 2.

6. *maquisarde*—In French, the word *maquis* traditionally refers to scrubland or bush. During World War II, the Resistance was referred to as the *Maquis*, and members of the Resistance *maquisards*. The term carried over to the Algerian war of liberation, and Zoulikha is therefore a *maquisarde*, a member of the Algerian Resistance.

7. See chapter 3 for a discussion on the transcultural space Yan-Zi inhabits after her death.

8. As discussed in chapter 2, Seigneur Nilou is the god-like figure Yan-Zi expects to accompany her to heaven.

9. Mokeddem's novel *Le siècle des sauterelles* also presents an orphan girl. Yasmine is traumatized by her mother's murder yet unable to cry for her. Like Kenza's, her mourning process is delayed.

10. In her interview with Yolande Helm, Mokeddem describes school as her "premier exil" [first exile].

11. The FIS, the Islamic Salvation Front, founded in the late 1980s, counters the secular National Liberation Front (FLN). The FIS has been linked to attacks on government targets and other acts of violence committed by extremists in the 1990s.

12. This phenomenon is discussed in chapter 2.

13. In *The Work of Mourning*, Derrida's essays on deceased friends teach us that mourning is an exhausting process.

CONCLUSION

Seemingly silent mother and daughter figures who cultivate self-expression in marginalized contexts have always fascinated me. Isolated from mainstream society or living in violent situations, women's voices of resistance, often subtle, surface in literature. *Spaces of Creation* took root in my curiosity about the links between mothers and daughters in the fiction from and across the French-speaking world. I identified a number of overarching motifs that relate to women's interpersonal exchanges and creative actions in the works of writers from the French Caribbean, North Africa, and Canada. In defining the corpus of texts for this monograph, I selected seven novels by six women writers. Published in 1967, *Un plat de porc aux bananes vertes* by Simone and André Schwarz-Bart treats many of the issues that would arise in Francophone literature of following decades: isolation, racism, questions of language, and sexism. Using this foundational novel as a starting point, I discerned thematic bridges between it and other novels published between 1972 and 2004. Each of the works demonstrates abundant hardship on the part of the female protagonists living in culturally diverse contexts. Nonetheless, spaces of creation inevitably open, making passages between women and inviting the reader to rethink the mother-daughter relationship from a larger and transcultural perspective.

Prior critical work on diversity by Edouard Glissant and Wolfgang Welsch informed my thought and enriched the present study. Glissant's commentaries on travel and life-altering encounters were indispensable as I analyzed the representation of women's relations with one another and their understanding of their own transformations in culturally diverse contexts. Welsch's theory on transculturality provided me with an inspiring intellectual framework that celebrated the individualized transformations that can occur in dynamic, lively societies. Yet I found that the work of both thinkers failed to take into account the issues specific to women in contemporary societies, for their exchanges are often less overt and free. The lacunas I perceived left room for me to develop and expound on a "feminine" transculturality that manifests in literary spaces such as family kitchens, funeral homes, and busy cities. To the wider body of critical work on postcolonial literature, my monograph contributes perspectives on women operating in restricted circumstances who find innovative ways to both tell about their lives and critique society. This "feminine" transculturality underscores the circuitous, often arduous manners in which women seek and find agency in culturally diverse contexts. Sometimes their voices emerge only after long sessions with persistent daughters or granddaughters. Other times mothers communicate through cooking, and still other times, women can safely express themselves only as spectral narrators. *Spaces of Creation* affirms that culturally rich or transcultural spaces are potentially problematic ones for women. Often fraught with tension and conflict, they do not necessarily conform to Glissant's and Welsch's descriptions of the vibrant exchanges that occur as one navigates societies, cultures, and languages. In *Le bonheur a la queue glissante* by Abla Farhoud and *L'Ingratitude* by Ying Chen, the narrators experience traumas that silence them. And in their quiet, mental spaces, they eventually begin to piece together the stories they yearn to share. In Gisele Pineau's *L'espérance-macadam* and Simone Schwarz-Bart's *Pluie et vent sur Télumée Miracle*, the empty home and comforting garden serve as spaces in which to first heal from and then recount the trauma of violence. In Assia Djebar's *La Femme sans sépulture* and Malika Mokeddem's *Des rêves et des assassins*, grieving daughters seek knowledge about their long-dead mothers through dialogue with women who knew them.

Of course, I am not the first to discuss the evolution of women in Francophone, postcolonial literature. This monograph added my voice to those of other scholars who have examined the trying experiences of literary mothers and daughters. I took to heart Maryse Condé's assertion that in some literature written by women, "every individual communicates with each other" (Touya de Marenne x). My study showed repeated and consistent efforts by women to connect with one another through voice and the written word. In addition, I strove to expand on Mildred Mortimer's notion of the home as a potentially "transformative space" in literature by Francophone women. Building on the work of other scholars and attuned to the tragedy of the physical and symbolic violence of literary mothers and daughters in Francophone literature, the present study unearthed critical spaces of exchange that women develop and negotiate in contexts of diversity.

These essential spaces of exchange problematize facets of transcultural, postcolonial environments. Their opening is gradual rather than immediate. The resulting interactions are intimate and attest to the shadowy aspects of women's lives, such as physical abuse and anger at being forced to leave one's culture of origin. *Spaces of Creation* revealed dynamic connections between the literatures of three Francophone regions, but there are wider implications of a "feminine" transculturality. Welsch's conception of movement and diversity are not bound by time or space. Likewise, the "feminine" transculturality detailed in this book surpasses Francophone Canada, the French Caribbean, and North Africa. Fiction from other parts of the French-speaking world, such as literatures of the Indian Ocean, will inform future scholarship on women's roles in rapidly evolving postcolonial societies. Broader implications include potential synergies between the present study and contemporary postcolonial Anglophone, Lusophone, or Hispanic literatures.

BIBLIOGRAPHY

Agacinski, Sylvaine. *Parity of the Sexes*. Lisa Walsh, trans. New York: Columbia University Press, 2001.

Allende, Isabel. *La Casa de los Espíritus*. Barcelona: Plaza & Janés, 1982.

Anagnostopoulou-Hieschler. "Espace féminin et image divine: vers une définition de la religion dans Pluie et vent sur Télumée Miracle de Simone Schwarz-Bart." *Women in French Studies* 3 (1995): 138–147.

Arnold, James A. "The Gendering of Créolité." *Penser la Créolité*. Maryse Condé and Madeleine Cottenet-Hage, eds. Paris: Editions Karthala, 1995: 21–40.

Ashcroft, Bill et al, eds. *Literature for Our Times: Postcolonial Studies in the Twenty-First Century*. Amsterdam: Rodopi, 2012.

Ashcroft, Bill. "On the hyphen in 'post-colonial.'" *New Literatures Review* 32 (1996): 23–31.

Ashenburg, Katherine. *The Mourner's Dance*. New York: North Point Press, 2002.

Badinter, Elisabeth. *L'amour en plus: Histoire de l'amour maternel*. Paris: Flammarion, 1980.

———. *Le conflit: la femme et la mère*. Paris: Flammarion, 2010.

Barbour, Sarah and Cerise Herndon, eds. *Emerging Perspectives on Maryse Condé: A Writer of Her Own*. Trenton, NJ: Africa World Press, Inc., 2006.

Bennett, Michael. "From Wide Open Spaces to Metropolitan Places: the Urban Challenge to Ecocriticism." *The Isle Reader: Ecocriticism, 1993–2003*. Scott Slovic, ed. Athens, GA: University of Georgia Press, 296–317.

"Bereavement." *The Concise Oxford Dictionary*. 9th ed. Oxford: Oxford University Press, 1995.

Bernabé, Jean, Patrick Chamoiseau and Raphaël Confiant. *Eloge de la Créolité*. Paris: Gallimard. 1989.

Bernie, Silvie. "Ying Chen: S'exiler de soi." *Francofonia* (Autumn 1999): 115–31.

Bhabha, Homi K. "Signs Taken for Wonders." *The Post-colonial Studies Reader*. Bill Ashcroft, Gareth Griffiths, Helen Tiffin, eds. New York: Routledge, 1995. 29–35.

Blunt, Alison and Gillian Rose. *Writing Women and Space: Colonial and Postcolonial Geographies*. New York: Guilford Press, 1994.

Bourdieu, Pierre. *Masculine Domination*. Richard Nice, trans. Stanford: Stanford University Press, 2001.

Cardinal, Marie. *Au pays de mes racines*. Paris: Broché, 1998.

Casteel, Sarah Phillips. "New World Pastoral: The Caribbean Garden and Emplacement in Gisèle Pineau and Shani Mooto." *Interventions* 5.1 (2003): 12–28.

Césaire, Aimé. *Cahier d'un retour au pays natal*. Paris: Présence Africaine, 1983.

Chamoiseau, Patrick and Raphaël Confiant. *Lettres créoles*. Paris: Gallimard, 1999.

Chen, Ying. *L'Ingratitude*. Montréal: Lémac, 1995.

Cheng, François. *Cinq méditations sur la mort (Autrement dit sur la vie)*. Paris: Albin Michel, 2013.

Cohen, Albert. *Le livre de ma mère*. Paris: Gallimard, 1974.

Colette, Sidonie. *La Maison de Claudine*. 1922. Paris: Hachette, 1960.

———. *La Naissance du jour*. In *Colette: Romans-Récits-Souvenirs*, Volume II. Guy Schoeller, ed. Paris: Editions Robert Laffont, 1989. 579–652.

———. *Sido et Les vrilles de la vigne*. Paris: Hachette, 1930.

Condé, Maryse. *La Belle Créole*. Paris: Mercure de France, 2001.

———. *La parole des femmes: Essai sur des romancières des Antilles de langue française*. Paris: L'Harmattan, 1979.

———. *Traversée de la Mangrove*. Paris: Mercure de France, 1989.

Dagenais, Natasha. "L'Espace migrant/l'espace de la memoire: Le Bonheur a la queue glissant d'Abla Farhoud." *Intercultural Journeys/Parcours interculturels*. Natasha Dagenais and Joana Daxell, eds. Baldwin Mills, Québec: Université de Sherbrooke, 2001, 2002. 125–139.

De Beauvoir, Simone. *L'Invitée*. Paris: Broché, 1968.

———. *Les Bouches inutiles*. Paris: Broché, 1945.

———. *Le Deuxième sexe*. Paris: Broché, 1949.

———. *Les Mandarins*. Paris: Broché, 1961.

———. *Mémoires d'une jeune fille rangée*. Paris: Gallimard, 1958.

———. *Une mort très douce*. Paris: Gallimard, 1964.

Des Forêts, Louis-René. *Poèmes de Samuel Wood*. Qtd. in *La Femme sans sépulture* by Assia Djebar. Paris: Albin Michel, 2002: 11.

De Oliveira, Humberto Luiz. "Migrations, Exils et Reconfigurations Identitaires." *Babilonia*. 2–3 (2005): 91–107.

Delvaux, Martine. *Histoires de fantômes: Spectralité et témoignage dans les récits de femmes contemporains*. Montreal: PU Montréal, 2005.

Derrida, Jacques. *Specters of Marx*. New York: Routeledge, 2006.

Djebar, Assia. *Ces voix qui m'assiègent*. Paris: Albin Michel, 1999.

———. *Femmes d'Alger dans leur appartement*. Paris: Des femmes, 1980.

———. *Le blanc d'Algérie*. Paris: Albin Michel, 1996.

———. *Oran, langue morte*. Paris: Broché, 1999.

———. *La Femme sans sépulture*. Paris: Albin Michel, 2002.

Donadey, Anne. "Francophone women writers and postcolonial theory." *Francophone Postcolonial Studies: A Critical Introduction*. Charles Forsdick and David Murphy, eds. London: Arnold, 2003. 202–210.

Emecheta, Buchi. *The Joys of Motherhood*. New York: Braziller Books, 1980.

Farhoud, Abla. *Le Bonheur a la queue glissante*. Montréal: Hexagone, 2004.

Farrell, Michèle Longino. *Performing Motherhood: The Sévigné Correspondence*. Hanover: University Press of New England, 1991.

Fisher, Dominique. *Ecrire l'urgence*. Paris: Harmattan, 2007.

Flem, Lydia. *Comment j'ai vidé la maison de mes parents*. Paris: Seuil, 2004.

Foucault, Michel. "Des espaces autres." *Dits et écrits:1954–1988*, tome 2. Paris: Gallimard, 2001. 1571–1581.

Gautier, Arlette. *Women from Guadeloupe and Martinique. French and West Indian: Martinique, Guadeloupe and French Guiana Today*. Richard D.E. Burton and Fred Reno, eds. Charlottesville: University Press of Virginia, 1995. 119–136.

Glissant, Edouard. *Introduction à une poétique du divers*. Paris: Gallimard, 1995.

———. *L'Imaginaire des langues: Entretiens avec Lise Gauvin (1991–2009)*. Paris: Gallimard, 2010.

———. *Poétique de la Relation*. Paris: Gallimard, 1990.

Glofelty, Cheryl. "Literary Studies in an Age of Environmental Crisis." *The Ecocriticism Reader: Landmarks in Literary Ecology*. Cheryl Glofelty and Harold Fromm, eds. New York: University of Georgia Press, 1996. xv–xxxvii.

Green, Mary Jean. "Simone Schwarz-Bart et la tradition féminine aux Antilles." *Présence Francophone: Revue Internationale de Langue et de Littérature* 36 (1990): 130–132.

Hallward, Peter. "Edouard Glissant between the Singular and the Specific." *Yale Journal of Criticism* 11.2 (1998): 441–64.

Harel, Simon. *Les passages obligés de l'écriture migrante*. Montreal: XYZ, 2005.

Helff, Sissy. "The Missing Link: Transculturation, Hybridity and/or Transculturality." *Literature for Our Times*. Ranjini Mendis et al., eds. Amsterdam/New York: Rodopi. 187–202.

Hirsch, Marianne. *The Mother/Daughter Plot: Narrative, Psychoanalysis, Feminism*. Bloomington: Indiana University Press, 1989.

Hugo, Victor. *Les Contemplations*. Paris: Flammarion, 2008.

Jamieson, Neil L. *Understanding Vietnam*. Berkeley: University of California Press, 1993.

Kalisa, Chantal. "Space, Violence, and Knowledge in Gisèle Pineau's *L'espérance-macadam*." *Discursive Geographies: Writing Space and Place in French*. Jeanne Garane, ed. Amsterdam: Editions Rodopi BV, 2005. 103–17.

Karnoouh, Claude. "Logos Without Ethos: On Interculturalism and Multiculturalism." John Lambeth, trans. *Telos* 110 (1998): 119–33.

Kesteloot, Lilyan. *Black Writers in French: a Literary History of Negritude*. Washington, DC: Howard University Press, 1991.

Laroussi, Farid. "Eloge de l'absence dans *La Femme sans sépulture* d'Assia Djebar." *International Journal of Francophone Studies* 7.3 (2004):187–99.

Le Bris, Michel, Alain Mabanckou and Jean Rouand. "Pour une littérature monde." *Le Monde*. 15 March 2007. Web. 21 March 2016.

Le Marinel, Jacques. "La Femme et l'espace dans l'oeuvre romanesque de Simone Schwartz-Bart." *Women in French Studies* 5 (Winter 1997): 49–57.

Lequin, Lucie. "The Legacy of Words: Mothers as Agents of Cultural Subterfuge and Subversion." *Doing Gender: Franco-Canadian Women Writers of the 1990s*. Paula Ruth Gilbert and Roseanna Dufault, eds. Madison, NJ: Fairleigh Dickinson University Press, 2001. 203–216.

Loichot, Valérie. "Reconstruire dans l'exil: la nourriture créatrice chez Gisèle Pineau." *Etudes Francophones* 17.2 (2002): 25–44.

Love, Glen A. *Practical Ecocriticism: Literature, Biology, and the Environment*. Charlottesville, VA: University of Virginia Press, 2003.

Mehta, Brendha. "Culinary diasporas: identity and the language of food in Gisèle Pineau's *Un papillon dans la cité* and *L'Exil selon Julia*." *International Journal of Francophone Studies*. 8.1 (2005): 23–51.

Memmi, Albert. *L'homme dominé*. Paris: Gallimard, 1968.

Miller, Margot. "Traversée de l'angoisse et poétique de l'espoir chez Malika Mokeddem." *Présence Francophone* 58 (2002): 101–119.

Moisan, Clément. *Une histoire de l'écriture migrante au Québec*. Montréal: Nota bene, 2001.

Mokeddem, Malika. *Des rêves et des assassins*. Paris: Grasset, 1995.

Mortimer, Mildred. *Writing from the Hearth: Public, Domestic, and Imaginative Space in Francophone Women's Fiction of Africa and the Caribbean*. New York: Lexington Press, 2007.

Moudileno, Lydie. *L'écrivain antillais au miroir de la littérature*. Paris: Karthala, 1997.

"Mourning." *The Concise Oxford Dictionary*. 9th ed. Oxford: Oxford University Press, 1995.

Nixon, Rob. "Environmentalism and Postcolonialism," *Postcolonial Studies and Beyond*. Ania Loomba et al., eds. Durham, NC: Duke University Press, 2005. 233–251.

O'Riley, Michael F. "Place, Position, and Postcolonial Haunting in Assia Djebar's *La femme sans sépulture*." *Research in African Literatures* 35.1 (Spring 2004): 66–86.

Orlando, Valérie. "Ecriture d'un autre lieu: la déterritorialisation des nouveaux rôles féminins dans l'*Interdite*." *Malika Mokeddem: Envers et contre tout*, Yolande Aline Helm, ed. Paris: Harmattan, 2000. 105–116.

———. *Nomadic Voices of Exile: Feminine Identity in Francophone Literature of the Maghreb*. Athens, OH: Ohio University Press, 1999.

Ortiz, Fernando. *Cuban Counterpoint: Tobacco and Sugar*, tr. Harriet de Onís. Durham, NC: Duke University Press, 1995.

Pagnol, Marcel. *Le Château de ma mère*. 1957. Paris: DeFallois, 1988.

Patterson, Yolanda Astarita. *Simone de Beauvoir and the Demystification of Motherhood.* Ann Arbor, MI: UMI Research Press, 1989.

Picard, Max. *The World of Silence.* Stanley Goman, trans. Washington, DC: Regnery Gateway, 1988.

Pineau, Gisèle. *L'espérance-Macadam.* Paris: Editions Stock, 1995.

————. *L'Exil selon Julia.* Paris: Editions Stock, 1996.

————. *Un Papillon dans la cité.* Paris: Editions Sepia, 1992.

Prieto, Eric. "Landscaping Identity in Contemporary Caribbean Literature." *Francophone Post-Colonial Cultures.* Kamal Salhi, ed. New York: Lexington Books, 2003. 141–152.

Rich, Adrienne. *Of Woman Born: Motherhood as Experience and Institution.* New York: W.W. Norton & Co, 1977.

Rogers, Nathalie Buchet. "Oralité et écriture dans *Pluie et vent sur Télumée Miracle.*" *The French Review* 65.3 (Feb. 1992): 435–448.

Said, Edward. *Orientalism: Western Conceptions of the Orient.* New York: Vintage Books, 1979.

————. "Yeats and Decolonization," *Nationalism, Colonialism, and Literature.* Terry Eagleton, Fredreic Jameson, Edward W. Said, eds. Minneapolis: University of Minnesota Press, 1990. 69–93.

Saint-John Perse. "Pour fêter une enfance." *Œuvres Complètes.* Paris: Gallimard, 1972. 26–27.

Saint-Martin, Lori. "Le Nom de la mère: Le Rapport mère-fille comme constante de l'écriture au féminine." *Women in French Studies* 6 (1998): 76–91.

Schulze-Engler, Frank and Sissy Helff, eds. *Transcultural English Studies: Theories, Fictions, Realities.* Amsterdam: Rodopi, 2009.

Schwarz-Bart, André and Simone. *Un plat de porc aux bananes vertes.* Paris: Seuil, 1967.

Schwarz-Bart, Simone. *Pluie et vent sur Télumée Miracle.* Paris: Seuil, 1972.

Sebbar, Leïla. *Sherazade.* Paris: Editions Stock, 1982.

Stagoll, Cliff. "Becoming." *The Deleuze Dictionary.* Adrian Parr, ed. New York: Columbia University Press, 2005. 21–22.

Talbot, Emile J. "Conscience et mémoire: Ying Chen et la problématique identitaire." *Nouvelles Etudes Francophones* 20.1 (Spring 2005): 149–62.

Thomas, Bonnie. *Breadfruit or Chestnut?* New York: Lexington, 2007.

Touya de Marenne, Eric. *Francophone Women Writers: Feminisms, Postcolonialisms, Cross-Cultures.* New York: Lexington, 2011.

Tuan, Yi-Fu. *Space and Place: The Perspective of Experience.* Minneapolis: University of Minnesota Press, 2001.

Veldwachter, Nadege. "An Interview with Gisele Pineau." *Research in African Literatures* 35.1 (2004): 180–186.

Walcott-Hackshaw, Elizabeth. "Cyclone Culture and Paysage Pineaulien." *Kunapipi: Journal of Postcolonial Writing* 26.1 (2004): 111–20.

Wallace, Karen Smyley. "Créolité and the Feminine Text in Simone Schwarz-Bart." *The French Review* 70.4 (1997): 554–561.

Warner-Vieyra, Myriam. *Juletane.* Paris: Présence Africaine, 2003.

Welsch, Wolfgang. "On the Acquisition and Possession of Commonalities." *Literature for Our Times: Postcolonial Studies in the Twenty-First Century.* Ashcroft, Bill et al, eds. Amsterdam: Rodopi, 2012. 3–36.

————. "Transculturality—the puzzling form of cultures today." *California Sociologist.* 17–18 (1994–1995): 19–39.

INDEX

ABOUT THE AUTHOR

Allison Connolly is associate professor of French and humanities at Centre College. She studied French and Spanish at Hollins University and completed her MA and PhD in French and Francophone studies at The University of North Carolina at Chapel Hill. She has written about the works of Assia Djebar, Simone Schwarz-Bart, and Scholastique Mukasonga. She is interested in the intersections of literature and the art of tea.

CPSIA information can be obtained
at www.ICGtesting.com
Printed in the USA
BVOW08*2126281016
466342BV00002B/8/P